"I HAVE CALLED YOU FRIENDS..."

AN INVITATION TO MINISTRY

"I HAVE CALLED YOU FRIENDS..."

AN INVITATION TO MINISTRY

Kevin Thew Forrester

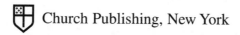 Church Publishing, New York

Library of Congress Cataloging-in-Publication Data

Forrester, Kevin Thew.
    "I have called you friends..." : an invitation to ministry / Kevin
Thew Forrester.
    p. cm.
       Includes bibliographical references.
       ISBN: 0-89869-426-4 (pbk.)
          1. Lay ministry--Episcopal Church. 2. Priesthood, Universal. I.
Forrester II. Title

BX5968 .F67 2003
262'.15373--dc22

                                    2003059633

Church Publishing Incorporated
445 Fifth Avenue
New York NY 10016

www.churchpublishing.org

5 4 3 2 1

Trinitarian Mutuality

The trinitarian arche (or rule) of God emerges as
the basis for mutuality among persons: rather than
the sexist theology of complementarity, or
the racist theology of superiority, or
the clerical theology of privilege, or
the political theology of exploitation, or
the patriarchal theology of male dominance and control,
the reign of God promises
the life of true communion among all human beings and all creatures.
Mutuality rooted in communion among persons is
a non-negotiable truth about our existence,
the highest value and ideal of the Christian life,
because for God
mutual love among persons is supreme. *

---

*Catherine Mowry LaCugna, God For Us: The Trinity and Christian Life, 399.

for
Rïse
Miriam and Liam

CONTENTS

℘
PREFACE

BY RUSTIN R. KIMSEY
FIFTH BISHOP OF EASTERN OREGON, RETIRED

This is a significant book by Kevin Thew Forrester. I confess to being a bit prejudiced in my assessment of the work as Kevin and his family are dear friends to whom I am indebted for wisdom and many acts of kindness over recent years. I am also an advocate and proponent for mutual ministry. So, perhaps I should not be taken seriously as a "prefacer" since I am hardly objective on either a personal or ecclesiological note. But I do want to write this preface, as I believe the book holds precious wisdom for Christians when a healthy theology of baptism is embraced and acted upon.

Kevin contends that the freedom and equality that mark the gospel of Jesus Christ are significantly bridled and blighted by an oppressive governance of domination within western Christianity during the past fifteen hundred years. As I read Kevin's surgical probes into the structure of the church over these millennia, I was struck by how seldom I have encountered such a relentless and, I believe, accurate critique. The church's institutional fabric has been difficult to target for reform. If Kevin is correct, and the primary motif of western Christianity has been one of domination by a hierarchy (usually clerical) more interested in control than in openness and equality, then small wonder that any cries for democratic revision of governance would go unheeded, stifled by the very processes that the reforms would have confronted.

i

For Kevin, the way into this prophetic challenge as to how the church should order herself is mutual ministry. As he states so clearly in this book, "It is the conviction of mutual ministry that baptism calls us into a community whose mission is to proclaim to the world that the hope of redemption lies in the liberation from all relationships of domination." Kevin advances this theme with expansive knowledge and no small amount of passion. On occasion Kevin's ideas remind me of a racquet-ball caroming off the walls of Christian tradition, analyzing and critiquing ancient ways of being the church and simultaneously introducing evidence from the gospel narratives and from contemporary leadership theory suggesting that the church's exercise of authority has been seriously flawed. The author even takes on one of the icons of modern leadership management, Edwin Friedman, and makes a credible case that Mr. Friedman, unwittingly or not, falls into the domination trap.

While his critiques of the past and present are helpful, I think Kevin is at his best as he revisits the experience of Jesus' focusing on the themes of freedom and equality, and reminding us that Jesus stitched together his gospel message of *no domination* while surrounded by systems of cultural and religious supremacy. Kevin strengthens his argument for an egalitarian structure of the church when he combines the Christology he has offered with his perceptions of how things work within the created order. Skillfully weaving the physical sciences, social organization theory, and friendship together, he audaciously makes a compelling case for a church that assumes unity, interconnectedness, interdependency, and mutuality to be common priorities in governance and visioning.

The chapters devoted to how you work all this out in congregations are perhaps the pivotal portion of the book. As one great preacher said, "It is one thing for Amos to say: 'Let justice roll down like living waters!' And it is quite another matter to work out the irrigation system." Kevin's chapters emerging from life in Northern Michigan are touchstones to assist the readers of this book to begin one step at a time into another way of being the church.

I served forty years as an ordained person in the Episcopal Church: six months as a deacon, nineteen and a half years as a priest, and twenty years as a bishop. In my ministry I know of nothing more important than the theme of this book—to do battle with any system of domination by a few, and to extend the understanding of call and ministry and service and friendship to all the baptized.

"Domination" often has a pejorative inference that one is referring to politics or control of circumstances or agendas. While I believe domination includes these matters, I am even more concerned that domination limits the revelation of God. When a community believes that a few have the wisdom to govern and maintain an organization without interaction with the constituency, something very dark happens: good, God-loving people defer to those who exercise domination over them, and all those baptized into the waters of equality and freedom are denied their legitimate prerogatives in their Christian world.

So, Kevin Thew Forrester's book is a significant book. As I retire from the active ordained ministry of our great church, I long for the ability to go back into my early priesthood and episcopate and focus on the friendship to which Jesus calls us. I reflect on how we might structure our life together in ways that make accessibility to dialogue more poignant. I think of how we might be more emphatic in honoring people for their ministry in the world, and how such witness might impact and inform the rest of the church in the spiraling nature of our life together. This book by Kevin Thew Forrester encourages my hope for the way I would like it to be.

ACKNOWLEDGMENTS

In his poem, "Some Kiss We Want," the thirteenth-century Sufi mystic, Rumi, speaks movingly of a kiss we each want with our whole lives. The wisdom we must learn is that to receive this kiss we have to "close the language door and open the love window." Declares Rumi: "The moon won't use the door, only the window."

There are many friends who have continually helped me to throw open the window and see within the light of the moon new possibility and new hope for the church. The words of this book draw their marrow from this lunar light and the friendships it inevitably births.

I hold dear my memories of working with Linda Martin and Sonja Miller of the Ministry of All the Baptized task force in the Diocese of Oregon. Through our research, dialogue, and explorations, many of these ideas initially came to be. Leslie Sackett, of St. Michael and All Angels, is a soul-friend, whose passion for children and youth continues to remind me that mutuality knows no limits of age. Church of the Four Winds helped to re-root my spirituality within the rhythms of God's creation. I am grateful to Jerry Drino for his willingness to have me present my thoughts on leadership and ministry at the Province 8 Commission on Ministry meeting.

Rusty Kimsey welcomed me without reserve as a partner in the development of the ministry all baptized persons in Eastern Oregon. His friendship, mentoring, and wisdom continue to pry open my window. The place of Eastern Oregon is especially "thin" for me, as the Celts would say. The congregations in Madras, Prineville, and Redmond in particular, embraced, challenged, and taught me, offering the chance to test and refine ideas of baptism, community, ministry, and friendship.

Tom Ray has raised a prophetic cry for over twenty years. His passion and vision are now of my heart. Jim Kelsey is simply my partner and friend in ministry development. Through our long hours together on the road, in the air, and over the dinner table, I learn and I laugh. Each month I gather with the members of the Ministry Development Strategy Team of Northern Michigan. Ours is an open circle of reflection, strategizing, and creative collaboration.

Two groups vital to expanding my vision and deepening my questions are Living Stones and the Ministry Developers Collaborative. Lynne Wilson, Eric Heidecker, Susanne Watson Epting, and especially Steve Kelsey, have willingly read parts or all of this manuscript at different stages of development, offering support and insight.

I owe a debt of gratitude to both Ben and Jane Helmer, who kept this work alive at a very critical point.

Linda Grenz of LeaderResources, in the end, is the one who brought the manuscript to the attention of Frank Tedeschi at Church Publishing. Linda has become a creative partner whose wisdom and tenacity are simply remarkable. Frank has been a delight to work with, even under the pressure of the tight deadline. Cynthia Shattuck's critical and creative eye vastly improved the original manuscript.

Finally, there is the moon, who is Rïse. She teaches me to see through eyes which are not mine, and so discover a God whose kiss cannot be forgotten.

INTRODUCTION

A few years back, at a gathering on the liturgy and the Prayer Book, I ran into an old friend and former professor whom I hadn't seen in years. After spending some time catching up, he said, "Kevin, after all those years as professor, working so hard to impress others with my writing and teaching, the one thing that I've become aware of is that none of it holds a candle to the friends I've made. When your life is said and done, it is the friends who matter, and none of the rest."

His are the words of the gospel of John. Indeed, his words flow from the heart of John's good news. Jesus reveals to us that what life, what community, what leadership, are all about, is friendship. "I do not call you servants any longer, because the servant does not know what the master is doing; but I have called you friends, because I have made known to you everything that I have heard from my father" (15:15). A friend is someone we know and respect, someone whose very difference we treasure and whose gifts we nurture. A friend is not a competitor, but someone we hold in mutual regard and affection.

This is a book on mutual ministry, which in many ways means that it is really a book about why and how the Christian community is a communion of friends. Jesus gathered friends about him from the start of his ministry. They learned from each other, argued with each other, betrayed and forgave. They learned that there is no greater gift than to lay down their lives for one another. So often the Spirit invited them to lay down their egos, which drove them, as in the story told of James and John, to desire to sit at God's right hand, rather than walk beside one another hand in hand in service of God's community of friends.

Mutual ministry is a way of talking about how we live in a community of sisters and brothers where leadership is no longer structured around a hierarchy of those of greater or lesser importance, but around the mutual nurturing of the gifts of all members of the community. In the Episcopal Church, mutual ministry has become shorthand for a baptismally grounded church, where ministry is not the prerogative of the ordained but is now "the shared ministry of all baptized people."[1] We can go so far as to say that to be a member of the community entails being a minister. To be baptized is to become one who accepts the call to serve others. Baptism and ministry are two sides of the same coin.

This shared ministry reflects the conviction that "there is *one* ministry in Christ and all baptized people—lay and ordained—participate in it according to the gifts given them."[2] Whether it be preaching, healing, teaching, parenthood, nursing, public service, or the arts, these ministries are the unfolding of our baptismal ministry. Ministry gives faith concrete and specific expression. I cannot serve Christ abstractly, but only concretely in my home, my workplace, my school, my church. No ministry, including ordained ministry, adds anything to our baptism. Ministry gives baptism its hue and texture—it gives baptism flesh.

Mutual ministry incarnates the belief that there is one baptism from which flows one ministry. This incarnation takes many forms, each orbiting around the central mission of the church: liberation from all forms of subordination and dehumanization. As God says to Moses in Exodus: "I have heard their cry . . . Indeed, I know their sufferings, and I have come down to deliver them. . ." (3:7,8). A baptismally grounded church has an Exodus character. God has come, is coming, and will come to set us free.

Our Exodus journey to liberation expresses itself within the church as the call to develop relationships characterized no longer by patterns of domination and submission, but by equality and mutuality. In *The Promise of Partnership: A Model for Collaborative Ministry*, James and Evelyn Whitehead propose "partnership" as the best way to understand non-hierarchical community relationships: "Partnership, both in the gospel and in contemporary life, is an experience of shared power. In this communal process, we explicitly reject domination of one by the other."[3] The church has no place for those who lead by dominating others. God has declared this Pharaoh dead.

It is important to explore some of the reasons for seeking to transform our churches into communities of mutual ministry. Since the days of Richard Hooker, Anglicans have affirmed that scripture, reason, and tradition are the threads that interweave, as in a Celtic braid, to form our common life. Scripture reveals a portrait of Jesus who proclaimed a "kin-dom" of God—a community where we all treat one another as kin, where we do not simply tolerate diversity, but treasure and celebrate it as divine gift. Christians are invited by the Spirit to form a community of equals, holding one another in mutual regard. Only by gently holding all creatures in mutual regard do we begin to gain a glimpse of the face of God.

The sciences also have much to teach us today about how communities of life, or "systems," organize themselves to survive and thrive. As Christians, we pay heed to these voices of scientific reasoning because they speak to us truths about God's creation. We live in a time of *kairos*, a time where we are becoming particularly aware how grace reveals a possibility of once disparate threads reweaving themselves into a new and beautiful fabric. Theologians and scientists have not always been in dialogue, but today the dialogue has resumed. Faith and reason are listening to each other with renewed respect, and the conversation is creating a fabric wonderfully revealing of who we are called to be as the people of God. Many voices from the new physics and the study of ecology tell of communities of organisms interconnected in a spiraling web of life that has no conventional hierarchy.

In *Spiral Dynamics: Mastering Values, Leadership, and Change*, Don Beck and Christopher Cowan explore in depth this spiral character of life and leadership. Philosopher Ken Wilber, in his many books, presents a convincing argument that the metaphor "web of life" is inadequate and instead conceives life as a spiral of transcendence and inclusion. He describes this as "holarchy," which captures well the reality of wholes nesting in wholes. Atoms rest in molecules, which rest in cells, which rest in organs, which rest in animals, which rest in communities, which rest in other communities. The whole is greater than the sum of its parts, which means "that the whole is at a higher or deeper level of organization than the parts alone—and that is a hierarchy, a holarchy." Science describes a creation in which all creatures are related and interconnected in a spiraling web of life. This web is neither static nor, as Wilber describes it, a "flatland" of sameness, precisely because it is holarchical. Each distinct whole transcends and includes another whole, resulting in an evolving spiral, with each whole being a part nesting within a larger whole.[4]

Scripture and reason thus come together to weave for us a new framework for understanding the third important element in Anglicanism, which is tradition. Too often, it seems, we continue to frame our reading of history in the misleading categories of ancient, medieval, and modern. We find ourselves speaking of the early church as if, by implication, we are the older, more mature church. Science, particularly the disciplines of biology and physics, insists we change our frame of reference. As homo sapiens, we are a species still in its infancy. This is even truer of the church: in future ages it is more than likely that our own present era will be seen as part of the early church. All of which is to say that the new framework of the Christian life offered by mutual ministry explored in this book is part of the struggle of a Christian tradition still in its youth, trying to remain faithful to its roots in Jesus of Nazareth, while heeding the voice of the Spirit blowing among us today.

This book represents my reading of some of the important signs of the times, or the voices of the day. They have something to teach us about our roots, and they challenge us to transform our community life so that it embodies and nurtures the gospel value of mutuality at the heart of Jesus' own life. The promises and pledges of the baptismal covenant found in the Book of Common Prayer articulate these core values of a baptismally grounded church. One of the more profound implications of this covenant is that each and every recitation implicates the faithful in a restructuring of church leadership and ministry. Every occasion we have to baptize a new member, receive a new member, or reaffirm our faith, the community reaffirms its baptismal faith. In this reaffirmation we corporately proclaim our oneness in Christ. We affirm that our deepest identity lies in the waters of baptism, and nowhere else.

---

[1] See Stewart C. Zabriskie, *Total Ministry: Reclaiming the Ministry of All God's People* (The Alban Institute, 1995), ix.

[2] Ibid., x. See 5.

[3] James D. Whitehead and Evelyn Eaton Whitehead, *The Promise of Partnership: A Model for Collaborative Ministry* (HarperSanFrancisco: 1991), 8.

[4] Ken Wilber, *A Brief History of Everything* (Boston: Shambhala, 2000), 66-70, 116. He is a prolific writer. Among his many books are: *The Marriage of Sense and Soul: Integrating Science and Religion* (New York: Broadway Books, 1998); *The Eye of Spirit: An Integral Vision for a World Gone Slightly Mad* (Boston: Shambhala, 1998); *Integral Psychology* (Boston: Shambhala, 2000).

PART ONE

BAPTISM:
EQUALITY & FREEDOM

CHAPTER ONE

Listening to Scripture

Over these past several years I have often found myself returning to the gospel story of Jesus' encounter with the Syro-Phoenician woman in Mark's gospel (7:24-29). More than likely this story is not a historical depiction of an encounter Jesus actually had, but a story composed by one of the early Jewish-Christian communities trying to figure out how it was to interact with gentiles. They composed the story as it is precisely because they thought it embodied the teaching of Jesus. All of which makes the story a jaw-dropper, because it is Jesus who is the one being taught. The teacher is the learner. The teacher teaches by having the soul of a disciple, the heart of a student. This is not a masquerade. The composers of this story realized that the Spirit of Jesus is the Spirit of humility. All of us are rooted in the same soil. This is a soil needing the waters of wisdom flowing upon us from those about us—especially those whom we have already judged as having little or nothing to offer.

As the story goes, Jesus has just left Gennesaret, where he had a tiring debate with some Pharisees, and perhaps his patience is wearing a little thin with his group of disciples, none of whom seem to be catching the gist of his message. He has come into the territory of Tyre and Sidon and is trying to fade unrecognized into the background. This is when the Syro-Phoenician woman, whose name we are not given, approaches Jesus. She falls at his feet and begs Jesus to heal her daughter. Jesus verbally spits in her face. Who is she to approach him? She is no better than a dog. "It is not right," Jesus says in words that cut through this Greek woman's heart, "to take the food of the children and throw it to the dogs." Dogs—this woman and her child. Now who is not getting the message?

The woman absorbs Jesus' degrading cut. She prefigures paschal death—being hung out to die in public, as a dog properly humiliated. She has no place to go and so she speaks her heart. "Yes, Rabbi, but even the dogs under the table eat the family scraps." It is as if she is saying, "You want me to be a dog, I can be it. I know who I am. I am my daughter's mother. She matters more than what you and the others could ever think and say."

How long does Jesus wait before replying? How long before his heart breaks open and he sees the destruction wrought by his own ethnic prejudice? How long before the wisdom poured forth from this woman's heart melts the fear surrounding Jesus' heart—before Jesus can trust one who is unlike him in so many ways? We are not told how long. The story ends simply with an astounding reversal: "For saying this, you may go home happy; the demon has left your daughter." You, child of God, are worthy of being fed.

We each have something to learn as well as something to teach. Freedom is born in the awareness that we no longer need fear the other. What they bring, what we each bring, is only a sliver of the larger face of God. We cannot help but be humble and accept the other, for without the other we cannot be whole, we cannot see God, we cannot know God, and we cannot love God. This is the humble soil of mutuality. We need each other to discover our own blindness, our own prejudices, our own beauty, our own way into God. Mark's gospel reveals a story of Jesus' own discovery, written by early followers to help remind them that we are to remain ever open to receive the other. A community of mutuality is a community free and open to receiving wisdom and love from all.

This openness and freedom sums up what many of the earliest followers of Jesus experienced in their new way of life together. Freedom to be treated as an equal, a partner in the new way of this prophet from Nazareth. Freedom to move out from under the shadow of domination that seemed to follow so many of them wherever they went. Liberation, especially from patriarchal structures, is at the heart of Jesus' proclamation of kinship, for now all are kin in the Spirit.[1] As we shall see, the term patriarchy covers a whole host of sins and sufferings. This kinship of God offered hope to the hopeless, by inviting people into a community where never again would they have to be someone else's servant or slave. Jesus proclaimed a new community of kinship that could dissolve the master-servant bond.[2]

The Kinship of God

The parables and miracles of Jesus reveal a healing and redeeming freedom as the heart of God's reign. Again and again, to our surprise, we come upon a Jesus in the Christian scriptures who persistently contrasts life within the community of God's friends with life in the natural family. Why? The answer seems to lie in the kind of family Jesus knew, which was a system structured around a patriarchal father who had the power to control and to dominate the lives of everyone else. This family and cultural system clearly defined who was dominant and who was subordinate. Roles were not fluid, but fixed.

This hierarchy was the backbone that held family and cultural life together. It is a courageous Jesus whom we encounter in Mark 10:2-9, who speaks of marriage as an equal partnership and declares that the woman and man "shall become one flesh." For this reason a man may not simply dismiss his wife as if she were a piece of property to be disposed of at will. In Mark 12 we come upon Jesus remonstrating with the Sadducees, who have asked him a question about the property rights of patriarchal marriage in the form of a story of a woman who is married to seven brothers: "In the resurrection, whose wife will she be?" (12:23) Jesus replies that they have failed to understand, in the words of scholar Elisabeth Schüssler Fiorenza, "either the Scriptures or the power of God, because they do not recognize that 'in the world' of the living God patriarchal marriage does not exist either for men or for women. They neither marry nor are given in marriage but are 'like the angels in heaven.'"[3] They are like the angels not because they are somehow sexless or genderless, but because patriarchal marriage is ended. Jesus' teaching directly opposes a marriage system that favors men at the cost of the full freedom of women, for any system that can only value some by debasing others is clearly not of the will of God.

The presence of Jesus in people's lives, therefore, acts as a sword to sever the ties that tether people to positions and lives of subordination. Once we understand this, we are able to hear the words of Matthew 10:34-36 and Luke 12:51-53 in remarkably fresh and challenging ways. Jesus, they say, has come bearing "a sword." In a similar vein, Mark tells us that on account of Jesus' ministry, "Brother will betray brother to death, and a father his child, and children will rise against parents and have them put to death." Evidently, the year that ushers in Jesus' life begins with a sword cutting those ties that bind us down and enslave us. Not all ways of being family are evidently equal in the eyes of Jesus. "Without question, the discipleship of Jesus does not respect patriarchal family bonds, and the Jesus movement in Palestine severely intrudes into the peace of the patriarchal household."[4] Jesus extends the offer of peace, but the offer has a definite cost. We are not to gain our power at the expense of another.

When Jesus speaks in Matthew 10:34-36 of families sharply divided from within, son against father and daughter against mother, we might think that he is referring to the strife that will exist between believer and unbeliever: This may not be the case at all: Rather, it is possible to understand Matthew's Jesus as making the same point we find in the Old Testament prophet Micah, who tells us that "the son treats the father with contempt, the daughter rises up against her mother, the daughter-in-law against her mother-in-law; your enemies are members of your own household" (Micah 7:6). The thrust of these passages is, as John Dominic Crossan writes, that "the normalcy of familial hierarchy ... is under attack. The strife is not between believers and nonbelievers but quite simply, and as it says, between the generations in both directions. Jesus will tear the hierarchical and patriarchal family in two along the axis of domination and subordination."[5]

A discipleship of equals cannot be based upon a family system in which only the father of the household is free and all the rest are possessed as servants or slaves. The patriarchal family holds out no possibility for becoming the means through which Jesus could reveal what kinship with God might mean. Servants and slaves are not friends, and friendship lies at the heart of life in Jesus. "I do not call you servants any longer," Jesus declares, "because the servant does not know what the master is doing; but I have called you friends because I have made known to you everything that I have heard from my Father" (John 15:15). Instead, Jesus lays an alternative foundation for common life, offering the chance for a new birth from which authentic community can be generated by the Spirit. Within the way of Jesus, kinship and family is now based upon discipleship and not blood.[6]

Even from our own vantage point today, it is hard to conceive of Jesus doing anything more contentious and subversive than challenging the legitimacy of the father's role as a dominant and controlling figure. Yet he does this by inviting followers into a community of friends that allows no place for the traditional patriarchal father. What we must bear in mind, however, is that the reason Jesus rejects the traditional family and father figure is precisely because he is pro-family, affirming *all* of its members. It is fair to say that Jesus lives and dies on behalf of a community of sisters and brothers who are to relate to one another as a "new 'family' of *equal discipleship*."[7] Here we have the ancient reason to sing the spiritual, "Free, at last, free, at last. Thank God almighty I am free, at last."

The gift of freedom does come with a price, particularly for the free men in Jesus' company. Will they be able to learn how to relinquish all claims of dominating power? Will those who have been servants and slaves all their lives not be seduced by the allure to become themselves ones who lord their new found power over others? Each and every follower in the way of Jesus is asked to be willing to begin life again as a vulnerable child. What is true for Jesus is now true for them, because they belong to none but the one Jesus called "Abba." Nothing states this fundamental characteristic of community life better than Mark 10:15: "Truly I tell you, whoever does not receive the kingdom of God as a little child will never enter it." This is not an invitation to childlike innocence and naiveté but a challenge to relinquish all claims of power and domination over others.[8]

Jesus' proclamation of equality goes to the very heart of the life he knew in first-century Palestine and seeks to reform it. He is not content to tinker at the edges. Either we live in a community where all are free to be friends, or we do not; there does not seem to be a third alternative for Jesus. As Walter Wink writes, "These are the words and deeds, not of a minor reformer, but of an egalitarian prophet who repudiates the very premises on which domination is based: the right of some to lord it over others by means of power, wealth, shaming, or titles."[9]

Jesus is a Jew from Nazareth who seems to think that kinship with God is open to nobodies like women, children, the poor, the deformed, and the ill. Crossan describes all Jesus' sayings that pertain to children, the poor, and the wealthy as sayings "actually talking about power and rule." Jesus overturns the power of the traditional family by proclaiming that with God it is the humble children and the destitute poor who have equal access to power and rule.[10] Jesus does not mean literally that children rule, but that kinship with God is open to children as well as adults. Jesus' embrace of children symbolizes that God's love excludes no one. If children have place and voice, then everyone does. Jesus effectively lowers the bar into God's community so that anyone might step in.

Nor does Jesus restrict his rejection of patriarchal power to the traditional family father figure, but extends it into the heart of the teacher-student relationship as well. Jesus is a teacher, yes, but he is no ordinary first-century rabbi, nor are his followers, his friends, to take on the trappings of conventional rabbis. In Matthew 23:8-9, Jesus instructs his followers that they are not to be like their own religious leaders who have people call them rabbi: "But you are not to be called rabbi, for you have one teacher, and you are all students. And call no one your father on earth, for you have one Father—the one in heaven." We are not only children, but students: the followers of Jesus are to be vulnerable and anxious to learn. What is at stake here for Jesus is the way his followers are to exercise leadership. The teacher is not a god who lords his knowledge over others. Jesus' followers are to lead by including others in the circle of learning. Before God, all are listeners and learners. "The discipleship of equals," writes Schüssler Fiorenza, "rejects teachers because it is constituted and taught by one, and only one, teacher. Similarly, the kinship relationship in the discipleship of equals does not admit of 'any father' because it is sustained by the gracious goodness of God whom the disciples and Jesus call 'father.'"[11]

We can find a similar sentiment in Luke 22:24-27, where the gospel portrays a dispute among the disciples as to which of them is to be "the greatest." Jesus tells them that unlike "the kings of the gentiles, . . . the greatest among you must become like the youngest, and the leader like one who serves. For who is greater, the one who is at the table or the one who serves? Is it not the one at the table?" The purpose of Jesus here is to reject neither ambition nor power. He seeks to transform the value system itself within which we desire and seek ambition and power.

To sum things up, at the heart of Jesus' teaching about God lies an alternative foundation for community life. One way to describe this way of life is to say that his friends are to care for each other in a spirit of mutuality. Mutuality will guide how they minister to one another. This community of mutual ministry offers the people a chance to start over again, a chance to loose the ties that bind and to trust the regenerative power of God's Spirit. To embrace such a way of life is indeed to be born anew. This rebirth is a redeeming passage from domination into equality, and as such it offers a taste of the fullness of life with God. God's followers will receive new eyes to see the family about them—a community of friends rooted in freedom. Freedom was the ancient promise of the God of the Hebrews who delivered the people from the foreign hand of Pharaoh and anyone other than God who might lay claim to own them.

I think it is now clear that the freedom offered by Jesus is not peripheral to his proclamation. Not only does Jesus explicitly call us into the freedom of equality and mutuality, this call is *at the heart* of our new life in kinship with God.

Table Companionship

I have spoken repeatedly of the words and deeds of Jesus calling us into the freedom of relationships of equality and mutuality. One of the central ways Jesus' own deeds expressed this call was through the practice of table companionship. There is good evidence to claim that Jesus ate indiscriminately with everyone.

He was not choosy. Or, to put it another way, he chose a place for everyone at his table. We find a description of such table practice in Luke 14:12-14.

> He said also to the one who had invited him, "When you give a luncheon or a dinner, do not invite your friends or your brothers or your relatives or rich neighbors, in case they may invite you in return, and you would be repaid. But when you give a banquet, invite the poor, the crippled, the lame, and the blind."

What are the implications of such a practice? As scholar John Dominic Crossan reminds us,

> To invite the outcasts for a special meal is a less socially radical act than to invite anyone found on the streets. It is that "anyone" that negates the very social function of table, namely, to establish a social ranking by what one eats, how one eats, and with whom one eats. It is the random and open commensality of the parable's meal that is its most startling element.[12]

We hear this simultaneous threat and hope for equality in the sayings that have to do with the source of defilement in our lives. In Mark 7:14-15, Jesus says, "Listen to me, all of you, and understand: there is nothing outside a person that by going in can defile, but the things that come out are what defile." Jesus presses the same point on the Pharisees in Luke 11:39-41 when he tells them, "Now you Pharisees clean the outside of the cup and of the dish, but inside you are full of greed and wickedness. You fools! Did not the one who made the outside make the inside also? So give for alms those things that are within; and see, everything will be clean for you."

The implications of Jesus' open table seem quite clear, even if they are difficult for his contemporaries and for us to heed. Indiscriminate table fellowship, eating and drinking with whomever we choose, is an offense in any culture where "distinctions among food and guests mirror social distinctions, discriminations, and hierarchies."[13] What Jesus is accomplishing through his table practice and parables is planting the seeds of an alternative symbolic universe. Access to power is no longer symbolized in the person of the patriarchal father figure, but in the person of the vulnerable child, the anxious student, the inclusive table. Jesus seems to abolish both rank and status, an action that carries submission and hierarchy away in its wake and leaves behind the beginnings for a community of equals.

---

[1] See Elisabeth Schüssler Fiorenza, *In Memory of Her: A Feminist Theological Reconstruction of Christian Origins* (New York: Crossroad, 1984), 151.

[2] See Edward Schillebeeckx, *The Church with a Human Face: A New and Expanded Theology of Ministry,* trans. by John Bowden (New York: Crossroad, 1987), 21.

[3] Schüssler Fiorenza, *In Memory,* 143-44.

[4] Ibid., 146.

[5] John Dominic Crossan, *The Historical Jesus: The Life of a Mediterranean Jewish Peasant* (San Francisco: Harper, 1991), 300.

[6] Jesus "abolishes the claims of the patriarchal family and constitutes a new familial community, one that does not include fathers in its circle." Schüssler Fiorenza, *In Memory,* 147 (See Mark 3:31-35; 10:29-30).

[7] Schüssler Fiorenza, *In Memory,* 147 (emphasis added). Schüssler Fiorenza writes that "Insofar as the new 'family' of Jesus has no room for 'fathers,' it implicitly rejects their power and status. . ."

[8] Ibid., 148. Schüssler Fiorenza argues that we can deduce the importance of this saying for the Jesus movement from the fact of "its inclusion in the synoptic tradition in a sevenfold combination, and in its transmission in very different forms and situations."

[9] Walter Wink, *Engaging the Powers: Discernment and Resistance in a World of Domination* (Minneapolis: Fortress, 1989), 112.

[10] Crossan, *The Historical Jesus,* 266;268, 273.

[11] Schüssler Fiorenza, 150

[12] Crossan, *The Historical Jesus,* 262 (emphasis added).

[13] Ibid., 262.

✌ CHAPTER TWO

Baptism: A Passage into Freedom

For the early Christians, to be a follower in the way of Jesus was to be free in the Spirit. Jesus' message of liberation was self-defining for the early Christian community, particularly for the Jewish-Christians who were dispersed beyond Palestine. To become a Christian was to become someone free to be equal, free to relate to men, women, and children in a spirit of mutuality. One theologian, Edward Schillebeeckx, has described these Christians who had been baptized in Christ as *"pneumatici"*—people living in the Spirit. "The God of these Christians," he wrote, "was and is the God who did not leave Jesus in the lurch after his death, but made him the 'life-giving Spirit.'"[1]

History is not perfectly clear on the origin of Christianity in some of these early communities. Whoever first brought the message of the risen Christ to the Greek-speaking Jews, it is certain that they were already living in the Spirit prior to Paul's arrival. The egalitarian spirit of Galatians 3:28, which Schillebeeckx calls "a kind of Christian charter of freedom," was not Paul's invention, coming instead from an earlier baptismal tradition.[2] Moreover, there are some indications that Paul was not completely at ease with the newfound expressions of freedom generated in these believers by the Spirit. There is evidence to suggest that some of these Christians took their newfound freedom to destructive extremes. On the whole, however, Paul was favorably impressed

---

13

with the faith he found, and his second letter to the Corinthians describes their way of life as one manifesting solidarity and equality "in the Spirit" (2 Cor. 5:17). Galatians speaks of people "living through or in the Spirit" (5:25; 6:1), as part of "a new creation" (6:15). What this language reveals to us is an understanding of community life that flows from baptism in the Spirit. This baptism acted as the foundation for community life.[3]

We are able to draw some general conclusions about how these early Christians saw their way of life. Baptism initiated the believer into a community in which all "were equal partners, without any domination in relationships." The waters of baptism washed away the old order of death and laid them upon the shores of new life in the Spirit. The Holy Spirit was the great equalizer who dwelt in all, the source of liberating power and wisdom in their lives. I think we can go so far as to say that Galatians 3:26-28 is perhaps the strongest and clearest proclamation of the new life that the Spirit creates. This charter of freedom reveals the primitive Christian vision of humanity reborn in the image of Christ:

> For in Christ Jesus you are all children of God through faith. As many of you as were baptized into Christ have clothed yourselves with Christ. There is no longer Jew or Greek, there is no longer slave or free, there is no longer male and female, for all of you are one in Christ Jesus.

Here we have Christian unity rooted in equality and mutuality, not in conformity and uniformity. Christians are free because they are equal. And baptism is the rite of passage bearing one into this new way of being family. It has been said that Gal. 3:28 is a declaration that "proclaims that in the Christian community all distinctions of religion, race, class, nationality, and gender are insignificant. All the baptized are equal, they are one in Christ."[4] In contrast to the traditional Jewish, Roman, and Hellenistic family systems, here is a community boldly stating that within its way of life there is no place for roles, positions, or structures that subordinate one to the other.

Another word for the traditional patriarchal father figure was *paterfamilias*. To the degree that baptism ushered all believers, including women and slaves, into a community of equals, it directly undermined the central authority of the *paterfamilias*. In contrast to Greek and Roman social norms, "early Christianity was a brotherhood and sisterhood of equal partners: theologically on the basis of the baptism of the Spirit, and sociologically in accordance with the Roman Hellenistic model of free societies, called *collegia*."[5] These societies served as a model for the early Christian house communities. It is no wonder that such communities proved attractive to both women and slaves. A Christian house community might be their only opportunity within a hierarchical culture to experience equality. Equality meant equal access to leadership. Much of the subversive power of Christianity lay in this possibility for women and slaves to become leaders.

These early Christian house communities acted to disrupt severely the traditional father-dominated household. Equality and leadership for slaves and women meant that these followers of the way of Jesus clearly broke the ancestral laws. They did not break these laws either lightly or by chance. Ostracism and death were always possible outcomes of such defiance. The Christian house communities knew exactly what they were about. They lived into their sense of equality in response to the Spirit's invitation. It was the Spirit of Christ who midwifed the birth of mutuality through the waters of baptism. We thus bear in our heritage the tradition of a Spirit-based family and community life quite subversive of the supposedly traditional Christian family.

The Problem with Church as Family

Mutual ministry also understands that the community of the baptized is called to be a community of equals. This means that however those in the church exercise leadership and carry out preaching and teaching, God asks that it be done in a spirit that respects mutuality. But what do equality and mutuality look like in practice today? Are they fine words, yet impracticable? How do leaders lead when they respect their followers as equals? How do teachers teach when they relate to their students as mutual learners? Equality does not mean sameness, as if all have the same gifts or the same wisdom. The church finds itself searching for images of community life and leadership consistent with its baptismal values. What kind of community life are we dealing with as members of the baptized in Christ?

Many within the American churches have found themselves drawn to the ideas of Edwin H. Friedman, whose *Generation to Generation: Family Process in Church and Synagogue* has had widespread influence in the United States and transformed how congregations understand themselves and their leadership across denominational and faith lines. At first glance, family systems theory does indeed seem to be a natural source from which to draw in order to develop an understanding of leadership for the community of the baptized. At the same time it is problematical, however, because this model both presupposes and perpetuates an obsolete family system rejected by Jesus and declared dead and buried in the waters of baptism by the early Christian communities.

Yet Friedman's influence remains pervasive within both church and synagogue. In part this is so because his systems thinking fits in easily with the church's own cultural and religious biases. Our own sin is always the very hardest to see. Despite Jesus' proclamation that all relationships of domination are contrary to the will of God and must end, the church too often continues to presume, in prayer, practice, and canon, that congregations are like traditional families in which the father is lord and master of the household. By "traditional" I mean to evoke the image of the first-century patriarchal family, especially that of *paterfamilias*.

To be certain, fathers within twenty-first-century households and congregations do not exercise power to the extent enjoyed by the earlier *paterfamilias*. Nonetheless, I daresay that whenever we speak of the head of a household or of a congregation, the first image which usually comes to mind is that of a father figure regardless of whether the leader is a woman or a man. Within our culture, both secular and sacred, such an image is like the very air we breathe. It is a natural, a given, which Friedman's work accepts. To study his writings is to come face to face with our own cultural and religious biases, where patterns of hierarchy and subordination continue to dominate our thinking. If we spend a little time with Friedman's work, however, we can benefit by arriving at a clearer understanding of the kind of community and leadership asked of us in our baptismal covenant. Freedom is born in such awareness, and as John's gospel reminds us, the truth will make us free.

Family Systems

Friedman believes that the traditional family system "presents an organic way of thinking that unifies our families and ourselves with the forces of Creation."[6] This system represents the will of the Creator, and as such, we should take it as our model for congregational life and leadership. Friedman asks the church to imagine the relationships among the baptized to be like that of a family system. He himself understands the family system to reflect the way God's creation simply is. That is to say, it is the way it is because the Creator God made nature that way, and human beings are a part of nature. How, then, does a church family system "naturally" function?

Friedman goes on to explain that the leader in a given congregation functions like the head of "any flock, swarm, or herd" that one would find in nature. Furthermore, every flock, swarm, or herd has its leader to guide it. Friedman argues that for an organization to be healthy and function at its best, it must have one or two people in charge, and "that is true whether the relational system is a personal family, a sports team, an orchestra, a congregation, a religious hierarchy, or an entire nation."[7] Thus the leader is in the position of one upon whom the herd depends for direction and, even more, for its ultimate survival. In this understanding of the church, proper control becomes an essential and appropriate expression of power in the exercise of leadership. Without the power to control a herd, its beasts could stampede right over the leader, as well as other unsuspecting souls. Without control, a herd could make off in a different direction from where the leader wants to go. Either way, without the leader out in front, the group and leader become lost. The leader's power to control the group is essential, for the group itself cannot correct its own imbalance or loss of direction.

To remain in charge amounts to a continual struggle to respond appropriately to changes that alter the life of the group or system. The leader seeks the right balance between action and response. The right balance brings the herd into homeostasis or balance. Why is this balance such a struggle? On the one hand, Friedman says, the leader can feel pressure to be drawn into and become a part of the herd. All of us can feel the attraction of this pressure to belong, which stems from the loneliness of exercising leadership from the top. Friedman describes this desire to transcend loneliness as the allure of togetherness. It is the inner voice that says, "If I could just be like one of the others, then everything would be just fine." If the leader succumbs, however, it can throw the entire group out of balance, for its leadership is gone. On the other hand, the leader can feel drawn toward a life of complete independence, which Friedman describes as the siren allure of individuality.

If the leader succumbs to either temptation, then the family or congregational system can become out of balance. Oftentimes this imbalance manifests itself in a kind of "cultic togetherness," which Friedman describes this way:

> What creates cultic togetherness in a family is *either* the leader *surrendering* his or her will to the group, which deprives the entire system of the leaven of individuation, *or* the leader *successfully exerting his or her will over* the will of the followers, and then using the fostered emotional interdependency to keep the family "unified." Where the leader's primary concern is self-differentiation neither of these extremes is likely to result.[8]

The leader's own self-differentiation is seen as the key to balanced and healthy community life. The self-differentiated leader is someone capable of recognizing both extremes for what they are—dead ends. Of course, such self-differentiation on the leader's part is no guarantee of community health, but without it the community is doomed. If the leader ever faces a situation in which the desirable balance must be temporarily sacrificed, in the end it is better to remain at the top by embracing individuality and sacrificing togetherness. In other words, if push comes to shove, a leader is encouraged to embrace control and sacrifice surrender. Freidman comments,

> Some may regard this as manipulation or as acting unilaterally. But if leaders want progress, in choosing between the poles of individuality and togetherness, they had better err in the direction of the former, lest they be the ones who are manipulated.[9]

Thus Friedman would have the church believe that togetherness is more dangerous than separation. This assumption contains an obvious cultural bias in favor of individuality that ripples out through family systems entire theory and understanding of community life. This approach fears that the leader will become lost in group togetherness without the ability to defend against manipulation. This fear, in turn, results in magnifying the importance of the leader's power to control, and in the extreme, even to manipulate those for whom he or she is responsible. Behind this fear and the need for the power to control lies still another assumption—namely, control is necessary because the leader is not able to trust the instinct, or good will, of a community. Consequently, the leader must be ever vigilant. The baptized community is always tending to go its own headless and misdirected way. It is misdirected because there can be no sense of direction without a top, the place from which understanding flows.

Functional Interdependence

The baptized community without a leader is "headless," which implies that the community has no inherent capacity to understand itself or the world about it. The community is "clueless" because, with this analogy, understanding does not reside in the body of the baptized. Perception, understanding, and wisdom reside elsewhere—in the head that must be joined to the body. The analogy does perceive a connection between pastoral leader and community in the sense that they are inseparable; the group needs the head in order to function properly. To switch to a computer analogy, the head is inseparable from the body as a programmer is inseparable from a computer. The kind of inseparability at play here is a matter of function, however; there is no organic connection. A programmer needs the computer in order to accomplish tasks, but the computer cannot understand the life of the programmer. Likewise, the programmer, or pastoral leader, cannot expect the followers to understand. He or she, after all, is the leader.[10] The function of communities, like computers, is to follow commands.

Clearly there is a relationship of interdependence between leader and community, but it is not an appropriate kind of interdependence for a community of baptized Christians. It is not an interdependence characterized by mutuality because it is not a relationship among equals. The assumptions of family systems theory preclude this possibility. To what degree the head is to be part of the body depends primarily on the choice of the leader. It is the leader who is capable of deciding to lead the herd as one might choose to program and run a computer. We seem to have reverted to a twenty-first-century form of the first-century, patriarchal household rejected by the early church in its rite of baptism.

This family systems model would have the church draw hierarchical lines of authority on the grounds that they are God-given, natural, and thereby the church ought to live in accord with them. The church is to accept this hierarchy as God's will for us. Consequently, this family systems thinking has made it quite difficult for much of the church to conceive of an appropriate sense of leadership and accountability that is rooted in the gospel value of equality. Is it even possible to reform hierarchy so that it ceases to be based on domination and is rooted in mutuality? The answer is yes. There are other voices emerging not only from the social sciences but from the physical sciences, and they have discovered a very different kind of community life—one in which all life is interconnected in patterns of mutuality. It is time to listen to what they have to tell us.

---

[1] Schillebeeckx, *The Church*, 34.

[2] Ibid., 37.

[3] Ibid., 35.

[4] Schüssler Fiorenza, *In Memory*, 213. See also William Baird, "Galatians," *Harper's Bible Commentary*, James L. Mays, General Editor (San Francisco: Harper & Row, Publishers, 1988), 1208; Sheila Briggs, "Galatians," *Searching the Scriptures*, Volume Two: *A Feminist Commentary* (New York: Crossroad Publishing Company, 1994), 218-236; E.P. Sanders, *Paul, the Law, and the Jewish People* (Minneapolis: Fortress, 1983), 177-186.

[5] Schillebeeckx, *The Church with a Human Face*, 47. See Whitehead, *The Promise of Partnership*, 4-5.

[6] Edwin H. Friedman, *Generation to Generation: Family Process in Church and Synagogue* (New York: The Guilford Press, 1985), 2.

[7] Ibid., 221 (emphasis added).

[8] Ibid., 232 (emphasis added).

[9] Ibid., 231.

[10] Ibid., 230.

♃ゑ
CHAPTER THREE

Listening to Science

When I lead retreats on mutual ministry, I often ask the participants to close their eyes and picture God. What they tend to describe is seeing an image of God as Father, as Mother, as Spirit, as Christ, picturing something or someone that is single and unique, much as when they imagine and draw a blade of grass or a deer. We have learned to treasure uniqueness and individuality, and in turn have become accustomed to fashioning a God in keeping with our own preferences.

Jesus, as a faithful Jew, would have begun his day with the opening words of the Shema, "Hear, O Israel, the LORD is our God, the LORD is one." And so *oneness* is an integral part of our Jewish and Christian heritage. However, as Christians in the West who are accustomed to beginning with one, we then find ourselves struggling to explain how the One can be Three. We tend to approach the mystery of the Trinity as a logical puzzle, which we try to solve deductively, beginning with the One. More often than not, we set the puzzle aside in frustration.

As we listen intently to the voices of science today, however, we hear described a picture of creation in which parts are always integrated with larger wholes. Atoms rest in molecules, which rest in cells, which rest in organs, which rest in organisms, which rest in communities. Science describes a creation in which all creatures are related and interconnected in a spiraling web of life—each whole is a part nesting within a larger whole that is forever evolving. Some characterize this relationship as "actualization hierarchy" or as "holarchy," which better captures the reality of wholes nesting within wholes. For it is only within the whole of our relationships that we live, move, and have our being. No creature, no person, is ever simply singular. No person is ever beyond or above or outside of this holarchy of creation.

The relational and nesting character of all creation reveals a communitarian approach to God, reflective of the Trinity. Creation as a system of interwoven lives leads us to affirm that relationship, partnership, and mutuality lie at the heart of being creatures of God. When we follow this communitarian path to God, it transforms our relationship with creation. We discover that to be a people sent is to be a people whose mission is characterized by listening, learning, and leading. These gospel virtues flow from a recognition and respect of the Trinitarian presence in all that is. The Trinity is not only how God is, it is how we, created in God's image, come to and rest in God. God is community and so are we. A theology of mutual ministry asks us not to begin with a singular one, but with a oneness birthed through the union of mutual love.

Let us begin then with the Three, when we talk of God, and ask ourselves, how is it that the Three are One? We are not questioning *whether* God is One, but *how* God is One. It in turn raises the question of how we, God's creatures who are created in the image of God, are one. What is it that unites us with one another, forming various individuals into a community?

In the fifteenth century Andrei Rublev painted *The Old Testament Trinity*, an icon of God that is extremely well known. As you gaze into the icon, you are drawn to an open place about a low table, around which sit three relaxed figures. Upon the table sits a cup easily reached by any of the three. Each figure rests peacefully and at ease in the presence of the other two. With heads inclined gently yet deliberately toward one another, they have a distinct air of mutual regard. A desire to drink in the presence of the others permeates the icon. These are figures ready to receive what the other has to give. Around this table each is utterly aware of the presence of the other, and each listens to the other with inclined ear and ready heart. One table, one cup, one mutual desire to listen to the other—born of eternal, loving recognition of the holy present in all. Competition and distrust are as wholly absent as trust and compassion are utterly present. These distinct three are one: one in open heart, one in listening mind, one in mutual love.

Rublev's icon is a vision for community life as well as an understanding of divine life. Mutual ministry begins with the inclined ear and open heart ready to receive in love the holy which is the other. Mutual ministry endeavors to embody in community life the same mutual respect eternally present in the life of God. The Trinity is a symbolic way of affirming the hope expressed in John's gospel that "all may be one, as you, Abba, are in me and I in you" (17:21). This is in no sense an exclusive oneness. Whenever and wherever we accept the Spirit's invitation to live into the river of love which sustains all creation, we dwell in one another. There is no love that is not of God, and so there is no unity born of love that is not of God.

The open and embracing character of Trinitarian love portrayed in the icon is revealed also through the warm space between the two figures in the icon's foreground. Here, there is forever a place at the table for another within the life of God. In a sense, God draws back to make space and then embraces, which might be a description of how God relates to all creation. Drawing upon the ancient Jewish doctrine of the Shekinah, the Spirit of God brooding over creation, we can think of the creation of the universe as involving a withdrawal of God to make space for creatures. God makes space for the emergence of a universe and for the evolution of life, and then embraces it. Trinitarian theologian

Elizabeth Johnson draws a comparison here with the pregnant mother: "To be so structured that you have room inside yourself for another to dwell is quintessentially a female experience. . . Quite literally every human person yet born has lived and moved and had their being inside a woman, for the better part of the year it took them to be knit together. This reality is the paradigm without equal for the panentheistic notion of the coinherence of God and the world."[1]

John's gospel declares that love is the Spirit that weaves our seemingly separate lives into a common fabric of community. Love draws a couple together to unite in partnership and family— united around birth and death, meal and story. These concrete and mundane activities are the very flesh of divine love lived. And love lived is the Spirit weaving wholeness and communion. If we attend closely to this reality, we not only survive but thrive, since wholeness is never realized in isolation but in community. Even if we are alone, our hearts are ever inhabited by others—they dwell in our memories, our stories, our hopes and sorrows, and we abide also in them. To live is to dwell in others as they dwell in us. God bids us dwell in love. For God is love, and we who abide in love abide in God and God in us.

As human beings, as God's own, we are ceaselessly drawn into community. Human history may be studied as more or less successful attempts to live into this call. The call is the voice, the nudging, of the Spirit who flows through and sustains all creation. The call is of God. We might go so far as to say that the call *is* God. Because to be God is to live in communion and to ceaselessly invite all creation to join in this communion of life. Trinity is not only God's life, it is our mission. The Spirit invites us to share the redeeming story that we are healed from our brokenness as we learn to live into communities (family, school, workplace, church) of mutual love and friendship that nurture our gifts and hold the promise of life.

Using Science to Re-imagine Community

We are searching for a vision of community life capable of transforming the church's hierarchies into a common life of gospel mutuality. We could describe our challenge as one of integrating the scriptural value of equality central to Jesus' vision of God with what I am calling a holarchical understanding of life, community, leadership, and ministry.

The new physics will help point us in the right direction. It tells us that the dynamic of energy basic to life and its evolution is fundamentally interactive, interdependent, and creative. What is more, this energy has the quality of chaotic freedom. It is through the freedom of chaos that the universe is able to produce, sustain, and evolve life, out of the very tendency toward stagnation.

If the Christian community can begin to think in terms of ecology and evolution, then it will discover that the concept of a holarchical framework holds great promise. Such a worldview can help the church achieve an important integration of the Christian scriptures' value of equality with the new physics' understanding of life's interactive and interdependent spiraling creative energy. This holarchical framework is more truly reflective of how nature works than the more static understanding presupposed in systems thinking. Creation is a spiral composed of wholes existing within wholes. Every whole transcends and includes another whole, which means that every whole is a part of some other evolving being. The natural diversity present everywhere within our universe reveals this interaction and interdependence. The dynamic of the spiral of life is such that each whole develops to the stage where it might transcend itself, becoming more than it was before, but still including what it was before. A healthy hierarchy works to make this transcendence and inclusion actually possible.

The concept of holarchy can teach the church to speak of human community, leadership, and ministry in terms of equality and mutuality, without a flattening sameness. We can do this while acknowledging both the continuity and distinctiveness of human community with other forms of natural communities or ecosystems. The faith community is a kind of open ecosystem where chaos and order have their own humanly distinctive expressions.

Such a concept can also provide the church with a means for acquiring a basic understanding of leadership and mutual ministry. It involves three steps. First, we need to re-imagine the interdependence of all creatures of creation, something we might describe as an ecological systems thinking. Second, since we may no longer draw upon the metaphor of the hierarchical family to understand the baptized community and its leadership, we need a new guiding metaphor. We will draw upon the image of the spiraling web of life. The image of a spiral helps us to understand that the web of life is neither stagnant nor static. Life is a journey, an evolution, of creatures-in-community. Third, we will conclude our journey by looking at a second metaphor, which is that of embodiment. The wholistic language of embodiment can help the church to transform the dualistic language of head and body so prevalent in conventional family systems thinking. Each of us is an embodied (whole) being, and so leaders are embodied in the communities they serve. Interconnected people are embodied people—embodied individually and communally.

The New Physics

Margaret J. Wheatley is a systems thinker schooled in the new physics, who seeks to draw out the implications of this new manner of science for organizations such as businesses and churches. She makes an important observation. "Staying put or keeping in balance are our means of defense against the eroding forces of nature. . . . Any form of stasis is preferable to the known future of deterioration." And yet, by "venerating equilibrium, we hide from the processes that foster life."[2] In other words, there is a tendency for the church, like any institution, to resist change. But this tendency is only part of the story. It is not even the most important part. What is the new physics saying? It does not speak with a single voice, but from the chorus of voices it is possible to detect a consistent melody that sounds something like this.

First, evolution. When we look out upon our fifteen-billion-year-old cosmos we see within our own solar system the fact of evolution. Evolution reveals that within the cosmos there is a gradual concentration of energy into increasingly complex forms of life taking place. But how can we account for this and continue to maintain the second law of thermodynamics, which sees all life beholden to the law of entropy? How can there be evolution in the midst of inevitable death? In Wheatley's words, we must learn from the processes that foster life.

The new physics in no way denies the second law of thermodynamics, far from it. Entropy does reign. But it does not reign in such a way that it inevitably produces only equilibrium, which for human beings, or any form of life, means death. Biologist Arthur Peacocke imagines entropy as a stream:

> Certainly the stream as a whole moves in a certain general, overall direction which is that of increasing entropy and increasing disorder. . . . However, the movement of the stream *itself* inevitably generates, as it were, very large eddies *within* itself in which, far from there being a decrease in order, there is an increase first in complexity and then in something more subtle—functional organization.[3]

If we focus on the stream of entropy but ignore the small eddies of life swirling about us, however, we are in danger of missing the big picture. Life, in all its glorious forms, emerges and evolves in tiny swirls of energy. The new physics has revealed to us that it is precisely because the energy swirls between our planet and the sun that eddies of life have continually emerged and evolved. The earth is alive and teeming with life in our solar system; it is a kind of eddy itself, because it is not self-contained and closed.[4]

Such paradoxes abound in the new physics. For instance, as an open system, the more freedom the earth enjoys the more order it can create. Of course, I am speaking anthropomorphically here, but the point holds. The more open a system is the more able it is to exchange energy with another system, the greater chance there is of eddies of life developing. Yet another way of stating this paradoxical relationship between freedom and order is to say that in open systems, or systems in which energy is free to swirl about, chaos actually creates order. Life emerges—literally, it would seem—from the chaos, from the eddies swirling around within the steady stream. In a strange but real way, for life to emerge requires the interplay of chaos and order. Chaos is able to create pools of life out of the very jaws of slow entropic death. Not only is it true that in the midst of life we are in death, but in the midst of death we are in life. This scientific (and spiritual) paradox is pregnant with possibility for understanding anew community life and leadership.

The new physics insists that at the heart of life is the paradox of order and chaos, entropy and eddies, equilibrium and swirl. Within the river of resistance to change, there lie swirling and chaotic eddies creating whole new forms of life. If we attend to the flow of energy in these eddies it will lead us into a deeper understanding of why systems, such as the church, not only decay and die, they also emerge reborn and evolve. As Margaret Wheatley writes, open systems

> don't sit quietly by as their energy dissipates. They don't seek equilibrium. Quite the opposite. *To stay viable, open systems maintain a state of non-equilibrium, keeping the system off balance so that it can change and grow.* They participate in an active

exchange with their world, using what is there for their own renewal. Every organism in nature, including us, behaves in this way.[5]

This is not to imply that there are no closed systems in the universe. There are closed systems and they may operate like machines, but they constitute a small fraction of the physical universe. Like our living and breathing planet earth, every human being, and every community to which we belong, including our communities of faith, are open systems. We live and breathe and dream and hope in and through our interactions with those about us. We have no idea of what may come of our daily contacts with one another. Are we not continually amazed at what life brings us? Our lives are a swirl of energy. The possibilities before us are virtually endless, so long as we remain open to what life brings us. The story of the wandering Israelites is apropos here. There is living manna to be found in the desert.

Interconnection

Arthur Peacocke is a renowned biologist and Anglican theologian. He points out that from an evolutionary perspective, all forms of life, current and extinct, are interconnected. Everything, plants and animals and human beings, live in "intricate systems consisting of many cross-flows and exchanges of energy and matter, of a labyrinthine complexity that has, until recently with the advent of computers, defied analysis."[6]

Here Peacocke is drawing upon the language of ecology to describe evolution. In its simplest terms, ecological means interdependent. But this is just a small part of the meaning we are after. Ecology sees the organism as inseparably interconnected with its environment. In some ways, to describe human existence as ecological echoes the traditional theological language of human beings as inherently social creatures. The English word "social" is derived from the Latin *societas*. In its root meaning, *societas* refers to the human custom of living in a *polis*—the Greek word from which we derive our English word, "political." To say that we are inherently social beings then is to affirm that we are political creatures. We are who we are because we live in communities with one another. To affirm our existence as ecological is to affirm in us patterns of interconnectedness that include but extend beyond the traditional concept of human existence as social. The patterns of interconnectedness reveal a human existence within a complex web of evolving life. Most simply put, in the end, all creatures owe their existence to the same stardust.

It is possible to say that human beings are social creatures, yet insist as well that we belong to communities primarily through choice. Indeed, this is the mainline political heritage of the United States. We think we belong because we choose to belong. There is much truth within this liberal political philosophy. But there is also profound error, both ecological and scriptural, if we hold to the sweeping conclusion that we are only connected to other creatures as a result of our choice.

Creatures of Connection

Creation's spiraling web of life is not accidental, as if we somehow back into our connections with each other and the rest of creation. Nor is the spiraling web of life created out of a vacuum by our choice. Ecology teaches that interconnection and interdependence precede and contextualize all forms of association. We cannot help but be connected. We are conceived through human connection, and as a species we have evolved from other species. For any creature, to act is to interact. Someone and something, in addition to ourselves, is always affected by what we do.[7]

Another way of describing interconnection, is to say that we ourselves are living ecologies. Microbiologist Lynn Margulis has written a fascinating account of evolution from the perspective of bacteria. Her remarkable theory has gone from "heterodox origins through grudging interest to triumphant near-universal acceptance today." To oversimplify her beautiful work, each of our own cells is actually a community of life with roots in the ancient bacteria of our planet. Or, as Margulis herself describes us,

> We are recombined from powerful bacterial communities with a multibillion-year-old history. We are part of an intricate network that comes from the original bacterial takeover of the Earth. Our powers of intelligence and technology do not belong specifically to us but to all life. Since useful attributes are rarely discarded in evolution it is likely that our powers, derived from the microcosm, will endure in the microcosm.[8]

An essential ecological truth is that all living things behave as they do only in interaction with other things which make up their environment. According to ecologists, every creature both acts upon others and in turn is acted upon by them. Every creature not only affects others, but is always affected by what others do.

From Hierarchy to Complementarity

It appears that there are also solid reasons to argue that ecological existence is fundamentally not one of hierarchy in the traditional sense. It is all a matter of our perspective. We could say that as homo sapiens we are "above" bacteria, for "our power of thought seems to represent more than the sum of its microbial parts," writes Margulis.

> Yet in a sense we are also "below" them. As tiny parts of a huge biosphere whose essence is basically bacterial, we—with other life forms—must add up to a sort of symbiotic brain which it is beyond our capacity to comprehend or truly represent.[9]

In the end, what finally distinguishes a holarchical outlook as liberating is the challenge it raises to conventional notions of hierarchy. As it is sometimes stated, we find ourselves confronted with the paradox of what can be described as a fundamental equality of those who are unequal. Although differences between creatures obviously do exist within any ecosystem, including human community, these differences do not make hierarchy necessary. To recognize that human beings differ in their skills and gifts does not mean that one of us is of inherently more value than the other. Rather, we can discover in the difference of the other an affirmation of complementarity. We need each other precisely in our difference. Each has something distinctive to offer which can, in its own way, empower the other.

The bias and language of hierarchy, however, die hard. Fritjof Capra, in his elegantly written, *The Web of Life*, helps us to understand the difficulty with language. He points out that since the early days of biology, the multileveled structures of living systems have been called hierarchies. He also believes that this characterization is misleading, because science has borrowed it from the concept of human hierarchies. Unlike the fairly rigid structures of domination and control characteristic of the latter, in nature what we find is more akin to a multileveled order.[10]

Capra offers an alternative to hierarchical structures that in no way denies variations in organizational complexity that we all readily observe in the kinds of life about and within us. Although Capra seems to dismiss the reality of hierarchy altogether, we can learn much from what he has to say. Instead of hierarchies, Capra speaks of networks, which he suggests provide a novel perspective on the so-called hierarchies of nature. All living systems at all levels are networks. He goes on to say that

> the web of life consists of networks within networks. At each scale, under closer scrutiny, the nodes of the network reveal themselves as smaller networks. We tend to arrange these systems, all nesting within larger systems, in a hierarchical scheme by placing the larger systems above the smaller ones in pyramid fashion. But this is a human projection. In nature there is no

"above" or "below," and there are no hierarchies. There are only networks nesting in other networks.[11]

As we begin to speak of networks nesting within each other, I believe we enter into a holarchical way of seeing the world in which the idea of difference no longer implies necessarily better and worse. Instead, difference can reveal complementarity, and within that lie the seeds for a sense of mutuality.

Diversity

Diversity makes complementarity possible. I am not relating simply to myself when I relate to someone or something else; I am in relationship with something or someone truly *different* from me. This diversity is not threatening, but is the source of my creativity as well as that of the entire system. Diversity creates the space within which freedom can flourish. Diversity does not threaten the system's unity or wholeness. Why? Because

> ecological wholeness is not an immutable homogeneity but rather the very opposite—a dynamic *unity in diversity*. In nature, balance and harmony are achieved by ever-changing differentiation, by ever-expanding diversity. Ecological stability, in effect, is a function not of simplicity and homogeneity but of complexity and variety.[12]

It now becomes possible to begin to understand more fully that from within a holarchical framework we value equality, freedom, and unity in diversity. What is also important to us as Christians is that these defining characteristics of ecology are consistent with both the central message of the Christian scriptures and our insight drawn from the new physics that human communities are conceived best as open, free, dynamic, spiraling systems.

These defining characteristics of equality, freedom, and unity in diversity go a long way to undermine the bias of family systems thinking that holds up traditional family hierarchy as natural. Holarchy presents us with a more dynamic and flexible image of God's creation. In the spiral of life, organisms are continually becoming what they are, not because they are isolated substances, but complex relational creatures. Any organism is unintelligible apart from the environmental network, the system, of which it is a part and in which it struggles to survive. Conversely, no system is intelligible apart from the very creatures whose continuous interactions make it what it is. If, in Capra's words, we are networks nesting in other networks, then we are relational creatures to our core. The implications of this simple affirmation are far-reaching for the church's understanding of community life and leadership, to which we will turn in the next chapter.

---

[1] Elizabeth A. Johnson, *She Who Is,* (New York: Crossroad, 1992), 234.

[2] Margaret J. Wheatley, *Leadership and the New Science: Learning about Organization from an Orderly Universe* (San Francisco: Berrett-Koehler Publishers, Inc., 1994), 77.

[3] Arthur R. Peacocke, "Chance and Law," *Chaos and Complexity: Scientific Perspectives on Divine Action,* Robert John Russell, Nancey Murphy and Arthur R. Peacocke, editors (Vatican Observatory Foundation, 1997), 143.

[4] The possibility for this emergence of life rests in the dynamic movement or interaction of the energy that constitutes life. If the earth were what scientists describe as a closed energy system, entropy and death would reign supreme. "At equilibrium, there is nothing left for the system to do; it can produce nothing more." Wheatley, *Leadership,* 76.

[5] Wheatley, *Leadership,* 78 (emphasis added).

[6] Arthur Peacocke, *God and the New Biology,* (London: Dent, 1986), 35; 55.

[7] Cf., Marjorie Hewitt Suchocki, *God, Christ, Church,* New Revised Edition (New York: Crossroad, 1989), 8-32. Suchocki states this very clearly: Existence is "a series of instances of becoming. This becoming is *through and through relational. Relativity is therefore constitutive of existence, and not simply accidental.* Becoming takes place in the *creative response to the past;* in this becoming, something new comes into existence. . . . *Relationships are the beginning and ending of each unit of existence.*" *God, Christ, Church,* 10-11 (emphasis added).

[8] Lynn Margulis and Dorion Sagan, *Microcosmos: Four Billion Years of Microbial Evolution* (Berkeley: University of California Press, 1997), 36. See also Richard Dawkins, *River Out of Eden,* (New York: Basic Books, 1995).

[9] Margulis and Sagan, *Microcosmos,* 152.

[10] Fritjof Capra, *The Web of Life: A New Scientific Understanding of Living Systems,* (Anchor Books: New York, 1996), 28.

[11] Ibid., 35.

[12] Murray Bookchin, *The Ecology of Freedom: The Emergence and Dissolution of Hierarchy,* Revised Edition (New York: Basic Books, 1991), 24.

CHAPTER FOUR

Leadership

Once we understand the implications of the new physics and begin to see ourselves as living members of the spiraling web of life, it brings far-reaching implications for the church's understanding of community life and leadership. Once we take up residence within this new metaphor, the truth of Margaret Wheatley's words becomes increasingly clear. The essential issue in life and leadership, she writes, is "not control, but dynamic connectedness."[1] The primary question every leader must answer does not have to do with whether or not he or she will be connected, because we cannot help but live within a spiraling web of connections. No, the question is one of awareness and response. A leader needs to be aware of her connections and she must decide how she will respond to and live within the relationships that make her who she is. How will she choose to participate in the spiraling web of life that is her community of faith?[2] Within mutual ministry, this is where leadership begins.

The metaphor of the spiraling web of life has the potential to transform the church's understanding of the baptized community and its leadership. It offers a context within which to describe the primary task of leadership as the *midwifery of gifts*. Leaders are those with the ability to foster and nurture dynamic connectedness. A leader midwifes a community's gifts from his sense of deep passion and conviction, trusting that the Spirit is alive and at play in the members of the community. A leader is always vigilant for the emergence of eddies of creative life. To exercise leadership within the spiraling web of life is to be about soul-forming work.

Intimacy, Passion, Trust, and Love

Parker J. Palmer is an outstanding Christian educator who describes the task of leadership in terms remarkably consistent with those we have already discussed. Leadership, he says, implies *intimacy*—knowledge of the one with whom I am in relationship. "This is a knowledge," he writes, "that originates not in curiosity or control but in *compassion*, or *love*—a source celebrated not in our intellectual tradition but in our spiritual heritage." The leader is one who seeks to reunify and reconstruct our "broken selves and worlds."[3] I think we can hear clear echoes here of ecological wholeness and unity.

The leader is also one who is passionately committed to the relational holism of the community. This passion is neither soft nor sentimental love. Palmer describes it as "the *connective tissue* of reality—and we flee from it because we fear its claims on our lives." A leader is one who acknowledges and *embraces* the reality that "love will implicate us in the web of life; it will *wrap* the knower and the known in compassion, in a bond of awesome responsibility as well as transforming joy; it will call us to *involvement, mutuality, accountability*."[4] The leader does not discover who he is primarily from emotional detachment and distance from the community, but through empathic connection. Paradoxically, an appropriate form of detachment is possible only through a prior appropriate connection.

Unlike Friedman, Palmer does not seem overly concerned that this love will absorb and trap the leader in "cultic together-ness," where the sense of self is overwhelmed and destroyed. Nor does Palmer seek to differentiate the leader by elevating him above and apart from the common community life. This is because he recognizes that love is incarnate through the values of involvement, mutuality, and accountability. Love implicates the leader in a "seamless web of mutual responsibility and collaboration . . ., a seamless partnership, with interrelationships and mutual commitments."[5] The church cannot begin to speak appropriately of detachment until it is first aware of the deeply intimate connections, which bind us all, and knows how to live responsibly into these connections.

Leaders are in love with the people they serve. Does not Jesus weep for Lazarus? Does not the woman weep over Jesus' feet as she tenderly washes them? Such service in love is a partnership in ministry. Consequently, leadership rooted in love develops a sense of authority centered on nurturing freedom and creativity. Love allows the leader to trust the members of the community and to work continually to expand the realm of freedom and creativity for all. We are no longer servants, but friends. In other words, Jesus sees us as creative partners in the divine ministry of redemption, one that begins to heal the wounds inflicted by hierarchy in all its forms.

The apparent paradox of systems that create organization out of chaos (what scientists conveniently describe as "self-organizing systems") is that the more freedom they enjoy, the more order they create. If the connective tissue of the spiraling web of life is love, however, perhaps this paradoxical self-organizing dynamic of life need not be a puzzle. As Christians, we profess that we are creatures of a creation that has been made toward the image of the triune God of love. Relationality is the very life of the one Godhead. Relationality is not threat, it is life itself. As Elizabeth Johnson writes in her study of the Trinity, "While the solitary God of classical theism is associated with a bare, static, monolithic kind of unity, a unity of divine nature, the triune symbol calls for a differentiated unity of variety or manifoldness in which there is distinction, inner richness, and complexity."[6] In contrast to conventional family systems thinking, the greatest threat to leadership is not cultic togetherness, it is futile and fatal flight into false individualism. It is to seek a separate top place where none is to be found. Mutual ministry transcends such vertical imagery by transforming it.

Such leadership is rooted in, and begins with, a basic trust of the community in which we live, move, and have our being. This means that within mutual ministry, control and manipulation are not the tools of leadership. Margaret Wheatley describes the kind of leadership we are looking for. "What leaders are called upon to do in a chaotic world is to shape the organizations through concepts, not through elaborate rules or structures." Leaders communicate "guiding visions, strong values, organizational beliefs—the few rules individuals can use to shape their own behavior."[7] Leaders call the people forth into creative freedom, trusting that even in the midst of apparent chaos, the community will responsibly self-organize.

I am not saying that there is no danger of the leader becoming trapped in the role expectations of the community. Isn't it possible for a community to entrap and betray? Isn't it possible for a community to smother and humiliate its leader? Certainly. However, within the church we have allowed a fear of loss of autonomy, which is only reinforced by family systems thinking, to ferment into a misleading account of community and leadership. This fear has become a justification for the perpetuation of a hierarchical system in the church, which is unable to accept and embrace a profound and healthy intimacy, mutuality, and friendship among all its baptized members, including leaders.[8]

Because this is so, the church usually does not associate the capacity for intimacy with the exercise of leadership. The current emphasis on psychological detachment, in fact, would seem to preclude leaders being intimate with the members of their community. The work of psychologist Carol Gilligan can provide some insight here. She has observed that in their stories of intimacy men often speak about the danger of entrapment or betrayal. They fear being caught in a smothering relationship or humiliated by rejection or defeat. Gilligan goes on to point out in contrast that "the danger women portray in their tales of achievement is a danger of isolation, a fear that in standing out or being set apart by success, they will be left alone."[9]

This fear is also quite real. Paradoxically, it describes the situation of so many male pastors as they exercise leadership from the top or from the periphery of their community. Men and women have been encouraged by the church to climb Jacob's ladder only to find themselves detached from the very community they are to serve in love. They are detached because they are not one among a community of equals, yet fear that to join a community of equals means, in effect, to be smothered. As a result, ordained church leaders try to form communities only or primarily with their "peers," clergy who are also detached from their respective communities. The result is the creation of clerical support groups for those attempting to balance forever at the top of inherently unstable congregational systems.

Embodied Leadership

The kind of family systems thinking we explored in the second chapter is filled with hierarchical images that perpetuate and reinforce a concept of leadership that is characterized by separation and domination. When such an approach is applied to the church, it takes the patriarchal images of our Jewish and Christian traditions and attempts to give them scientific legitimacy. The language of domination hierarchy and dualism thoroughly colors this family systems understanding of the relationship of the ordained leader to the lay congregation. Author Judith V. Jordan notes that most work settings, with their emphasis on productivity and competition, are not conducive to mutuality. In such a system, she writes, "Hierarchy and lines of individual power and dominance are developed as incentives to individual achievement, but the inevitable interdependence that underlies any institutional power structure is devalued."[10] Such organizational thinking includes parish and diocesan life as well. With the spiraling web of life as the metaphor shaping the church's understanding of community, however, mutual ministry is in a position to rethink how we draw upon the language of body to understand leadership consistent with the baptismal covenant.

If you recall, the work of Edwin Friedman places the leader in the position at the top of the system. He consistently employs the analogy of the head and body to flesh out the meaning of being at the top. Such language is more consistent with a computer-based systems approach than a truly organic, or ecological, way of understanding community life. A computer, as Friedman notes, always requires the presence of the human mind to think meaning-fully about what is at hand.[11] It is mind that the head, as the leader, brings to the system. The implication for the congregational system and leadership is clerical domination. Leadership and mind are located in the one or two clergy at the top. The rest, the body of the baptized below, are not of the mind. They simply accept the spiritual rule of the clergy. From the beginning, Friedman's thinking tends toward a severance of the body of the baptized.

Furthermore, this family systems approach makes it necessary for the clerical leader to remain ever vigilant to avoid being manipulated by those beneath. Mind over matter is not an abstract principle here. The community's and leader's survival are at stake. The clerical mind guides the system as a programmer who has decided to work with this particular congregation. In the end, clergy are independent of the systems they guide. This situation is most clear in the language the church uses to describe a congregation without a rector: the parish is said to be "vacant," waiting for a new rector to assume headship of the community.

The church conventionally assumes that the clerical leader is a professional outsider come to lead a vacant lay community. We say that the community calls, but it is actually the leader who chooses whether or not to belong to this particular body of faith. If the rector belongs, it is as a ruler extrinsically connected to the body of faithful. From the perspective of mutual ministry, we would say that such conventional rectors have assumed the role of headship—but headship is not the same as baptismal leadership.

In *The Promise of Partnership,* James and Evelyn Whitehead have developed an alternative understanding of leadership within a model of mutuality that is more consistent with holarchical thinking. In their discussion of how leaders gain legitimacy, they write that "organizations may assign *headship*, but groups make *leaders*. They do this by accepting the *right* of the designated person to influence their lives."[12] The point they are making is that baptismal leadership is rooted in the life of the community and embodied in the living out of relationships of mutuality.

Similarly, with respect to the understanding of embodiment to be found in the Hebrew scriptures, theologian Jürgen Moltmann observes that the Old Testament offers not theological definitions but stories. The narratives of the Bible present the human being "in the relationships in which he lives." Moltmann argues, therefore, that "a relationship of community, partnership and mutual influence" is far closer to biblical notions of what it means to be human:

> The unity of soul and body, what is inward and what is outward, the centre and the periphery of the human being is to be comprehended in the forms of covenant, community, reciprocity, a mutual encircling, regard, agreement, harmony and friendship.[13]

At the same time, a tendency toward dualism in the Christian scriptures can undermine the radical vision of equality spoken of in Galatians 3:26-28. Christian ethicist James Nelson has described this tendency in a way helpful to our discussion. He points out that dualism, if unchecked, can transform creative tension into separation, domination, and control. This can manifest itself particularly in the church language of mind over body, spirit over matter, clerical over lay.[14] Therefore true leaders are those who exercise authority as embodied members of a community. Within mutual ministry, congregations do not search for those willing to assume headship—either as local leaders or as missioners. They call forth leaders from the local community of faith and they call missioners to mentor local communities. Mentors lead by listening, learning, and nurturing. All this is to say that leadership and embodiment go hand in hand.

Consequently, when the church draws upon family systems thinking to define community life and leadership, it only serves to reinforce the church's conventional hierarchical model. Freedom is born, in large part, through our awareness of our own brokenness and the powers that perpetuate it. Family systems thinking has worked to justify a clerical head struggling to lead and control the lay body, strengthening our prejudice of relating head to body as dominant to subordinate. It not only assumes this form of interrelatedness between leader and community, it argues that it is an organic phenomenon normative for our understanding of faith community. In the end, such family systems thinking sanctifies the very hierarchical dualism which continues to compromise the baptismal value of equality. It helps the church justify its separation and subordination of the lay from the ordained, which violates the unity established in our baptismal covenant.[15]

The metaphor of Christian community as a spiraling web of life moves mutual ministry to imagine the leader as one of many embodied selves rooted and embodied within the community of the baptized. If we take this metaphor seriously, we do not speak of a person as "having" a body. A body is not something we own.

Mutual ministry does not speak of a cleric having a congregation. A community is not an object of possession. "We are bodies." We are embodied words, embodied minds, and embodied communities—the body of Christ. We are the word of love become flesh and bones. And love has become incarnate not as isolated individuals, but as communities of faith. Community is the communion of embodied minds, or spirits. The Spirit of equality and mutuality is the warp and woof of this community life. In the words of Nelson, we are a people whose deepest desire is "for the expression of communion—of the self with other body-selves and with God."[16] We are a people who long for intimacy, above all within the body of Christ. As Christians, communion is our path to wholeness, and to unity in diversity.

It remains important for the leadership of a community to have a healthy sense of self. But as one psychologist describes the process of self-differentiation, it is not a developmental goal of difference and separateness. If this were the goal, then the church would be right back at the place of affirming that we can become healthy selves in the end primarily through separation. The holarchical framework understands the path to differentiation and healthy self to be through healthy and intimate relationships within the baptized community.

One way of speaking about this path to wholeness is in terms of relationship-differentiation. Ecologically speaking, differentiation points to a "dynamic process that encompasses increasing levels of complexity, structure, and articulation *within the context of human bonds and attachments*."[17] What this adds up to saying is that a leader acquires a healthy sense of identity only from within the bonds of empathy holding the members of the community together. I know how I am both alike and different from members of my community because I am in communion with them. Such communion is not absorption. Paradoxically, it is "an experience of unity but not unification. Each self respects the other's identity, not confusing it with its own wishes or fantasies."[18]

Let me draw these thoughts together by means of an image. The spiraling web of life metaphor can guide the church in the formation of a new synthesis, drawing upon two very distinct images: the differentiated rungs of a ladder and the equality of a circle. The spiraling web of life incorporates the insight of transcendence captured in the image of the ladder, but it transforms the rungs into a living and journeying circle—an evolving spiral. There is transcendence and development, but the Spirit of equality animates the spiral, and acts continually to embrace, shape and reshape all leadership and ministry. Self-differentiation is self-preservation within a community of equals. But mutuality, not hierarchy, is the standard against which the church needs to gauge a healthy sense of self.

Mutual Ministry: Discipleship of Equals

Family systems thinking asks the church to conform to a universal norm of what a clergyperson will do and be in a denomination. According to this norm, which the church knows so well, we are to set clergy, as leaders, apart from the baptized. If they are to have friends, it is not to be with baptized members of their community, but with other professional clerics. Proper boundaries are at stake here. It is as if boundaries, not friendship, have become the value central to Jesus' reign of God. (And as Ken Wilber reminds us, every boundary is, in the end, another battle line.)[19] Although relationships of domination tend to be the norm for conventional hierarchy, such a norm is at odds with the gospel and the baptismal covenant.

Mutual ministry has struggled long and hard with this conventional universal norm. Faithfulness to the baptismal covenant, and the church's faithfulness as well to the kind of creation our Creator has given to us, leads us to critique our inheritance. For example, one study has identified three major tensions in the lives of women pastors who struggle with the church's entrenched vision of hierarchy. First, women pastors prefer not to be set apart from their community of faith, for it is within this very community that they develop relationships among those who share their baptism and commitments. This emphasis on relationality is a new style in ministry, which comes in part because of these women's emphasis on nurturance and on relationships over functions. Second, women desire to return the sacraments to their communal function, with emphasis on the baptism of all members for ministry and the need to equip the saints through teaching and preaching. Third, these women's self-image is that of embodied pastors, rather than leaders who are separated and thus isolated from their communities.[20]

These three areas of tension reveal the need to transform the church structures that divide clergy from people and obscure the meaning of ministry as the work of Christ that is shared by all those who are united with Christ through baptism. The work of feminist theologians such as Lettie Russell and Rosemary Radford Ruether has contributed to the creative stirring of the Spirit that is moving all of us, male and female, to transform the church as we know it.[21] These tensions embody the Spirit's invitation to move out of a family system of clerical caste and into a new kind of family, a baptismal community of equals who share a variety of ministries—liturgists, teachers, administrators, community organizers, and spiritual counselors. Each ministry is a whole, resting in the whole of the community of which it is a part. This is the baptismal invitation to reform toward mutual ministry.

A holarchical approach to community helps the church to integrate leadership, in its myriad forms, within the spiraling web of community life. All leaders, regardless of the size of the community of faith, are equal disciples (in whom God is wholly present) within this spiraling web of life, called into mutual ministry through the sacrament of baptism. This theology of community and leadership ushers the church into the very heart of Christ's liberating good news of an alternative community. The theological undergirding of mutual ministry is the gospel's call inviting the church into a discipleship of equals through the sacrament of baptism. Commitment, accountability, and solidarity are the life-praxis of this community.

It is the conviction of mutual ministry that baptism calls us into a community whose mission is to proclaim to the world that the hope of redemption lies in the liberation from all relationships of domination. Baptism calls the church into a community in which leadership is characterized by the way in which all members of the community are participants in the decision-making process. A community of equals calls us to a restructuring of leadership. This restructuring is inspired by our Trinitarian faith, which reflects and embodies the message of Jesus of Nazareth. The church cannot divine what Jesus' intention was with regard to the foundation and structure of a community of faith. But, as it has been said, the more important question is whether the church today is able to carry on the mission and ministry of Jesus.[22] Mutual ministry proclaims to the church at large that we cannot carry on this mission and ministry without wonderful and creative variety from community to community, from diocese to diocese. This variety results from the many different gifts of the Spirit that are birthed in our faith communities

Mutual ministry does not invite the church to reduplicate any particular social or political order. The church needs to resist the inclination to reduce mutual ministry to a system, a model, a program, or order. It is a vision of a new way of community life rooted in the baptismal covenant of a community of equals. As Stewart Zabriskie, former bishop of Nevada, writes, mutual ministry is best described by "images that suggest mutuality, equality of order, the sharing of gifts and energy in and as community."

Mutual ministry is neither a "model to sell" nor a "system as the word is traditionally used. It is the acceptance of an inspiration, and Jesus Christ is the Good News at its center."[23]

If mutual ministry is neither a model nor a system, but the acceptance of an inspiration, what is it inspiring the church to co-create with the Spirit? There are many places to turn to discover this inspiration at work in our Anglican Communion. The international group, *Living Stones*, begun in 1994, has well over twenty member dioceses. Each diocese has felt inspired to respond to the Spirit somewhat differently, depending upon its local circumstances. Such differences reflect the reality of incarnation. God works with what is at hand, and we work with what God is giving to us. Gifts given and gifts received vary from place to place, but what does not vary is the commitment of dioceses to the ministry of all the baptized.

It is now time to turn to the story of one diocese's journey into mutual ministry.

---

[1] Erich Jantsch, *Self-Organizing Universe: Scientific and Human Implications of the Emerging Paradigm of Evolution* (Pergamon Press, 1980), 196.

[2] See Wheatley, *Leadership*, 23.

[3] Parker J. Palmer, *To Know as We Are Known: Education as a Spiritual Journey* (San Francisco: HarperSanFrancisco, 1993), 8 (emphasis added).

[4] Ibid., 9 (emphasis added).

[5] Robert Howard, "Values Make the Company: An Interview with Robert Haas," *Harvard Business Review* (Sept-Oct, 1990): 136. See Wheatley, *Leadership*, 140.

[6] Elizabeth A. Johnson, *She Who Is: The Mystery of God in Feminist Theological Discourse* (New York: Crossroad, 1992), 219.

[7] Wheatley, *Leadership*, 133.

[8] See Lynn N. Rhodes, *Co-Creating: A Feminist Vision of Ministry, "Feminist Ministry: Vision of Friendship and Solidarity"* (Philadelphia: The Westminster Press, 1987), 122-127.

[9] Carol Gilligan, *In a Different Voice: Psychological Theory and Women's Development* (Cambridge, Mass: Harvard University Press, 1982), 42.

[10] Judith V. Jordan, "The Meaning of Mutuality" in Jordan, *Women's Growth*, 94.

[11] Friedman, *Generation to Generation*, 15.

---

[12] Whitehead, *The Promise of Partnership,* 66, 65. The Whiteheads point out that it is in and through the interplay of institutional, personal, and extra-rational (that is to say, the "symbolic role of the leader" and "religious authenticity") factors that one gains leadership.

[13] Moltmann, *God in Creation* (Minneapolis: Fortress Press, 1993), 256-58.

[14] James B. Nelson, *Body Theology* (Louisville, Kentucky: Westminster/John Knox Press, 1992), 22; 44; 113.

[15] For a fuller discussion, see James B. Nelson's works, *The Intimate Connection: Male Sexuality, Masculine Spirituality* (Philadelphia: The Westminster Press, 1988) and *Embodiment: An Approach to Sexuality and Christian Theology* (Minneapolis: Augsburg, 1978); Sallie McFague, *Models of God: Theology for an Ecological, Nuclear Age* (Philadelphia: Fortress Press, 1987)

[16] Nelson, *Body Theology,* 43, 52.

[17] Surrey, "The Relational Self in Women," Jordan, *Women's Growth,* 36 (emphasis added). See also "The Self-in-Relation: A Theory of Women's Development," 60-61, as well as Catherine Keller, *From a Broken Web: Separation, Sexism, and Self* (Boston: Beacon Press, 1986), 136-140.

[18] Nelson, *Embodiment,* 34, 35. See Nelson, *The Intimate Connection,* 26.

[19] See Ken Wilber, *No Boundary: Eastern and Western Approaches to Personal Growth* (Shambhala: Boston, 2001).

[20] Barbara Brown Zikmund, "Changing Understandings of Ordination," in *The Presbyterian Predicament: Six Perspectives,* ed. Milton J. Coalter, John M. Mulder, and Louis B. Weeks (Louisville, Kentucky: Westminster/John Knox Press, 1990), 149-158.

[21] See Letty M. Russell, *Church in the Round: Feminist Interpretation of the Church* (Louisville, Kentucky: Westminster/John Knox Press, 1993), 52-53, and Rosemary Radford Ruether, *Women-Church: Theology and Practice of Feminist Liturgical Communities* (San Francisco: Harper & Row, 1985), 87-91.

[22] See Mary E. Hines, "Community For Liberation," *Freeing Theology: The Essentials of Theology in Feminist Perspective,* Catherine Mowry LaCugna, Editor (New York: HarperCollins, 1993), 171. See Francis Schüssler Fiorenza, *Foundational Theology: Jesus and the Church* (New York: Crossroad, 1984), 108-22, 168; Edward Schillebeeckx, *Church: The Human Story of God,* trans. John Bowden (New York: Crossroad, 1990), 230-231.

[23] Zabriskie, *Total Ministry,* 1-2.

PART TWO

A PEOPLE TRANSFORMED THROUGH MUTUAL MINISTRY

Now is the time to know
That all you do is sacred.
Now, why not consider
A lasting truce with yourself and God.
Now is the time to understand
That all your ideas of right and wrong
Were just a child's training wheels
To be laid aside
When you can finally live
With veracity
And love.
Hafiz is a divine envoy
Whom the Beloved
Has written a holy message upon.
My dear, please tell me,
Why do you still
Throw sticks at your heart
And God?
What is it in that sweet voice inside
That incites you to fear?
Now is the time for the world to know
That every thought and action is sacred.
This is the time for you to compute the impossibility
That there is anything
But Grace.
Now is the season to know
That everything you do
Is sacred.[1]

ぺの
CHAPTER FIVE

How to Set a Table in the Wilderness

The Diocese of Northern Michigan commenced its journey into mutual ministry in the mid-1980s, when several disparate threads came together and made possible the weaving of a new way of being church in the Upper Peninsula of the state. These disparate threads included the remote and rural geography of the Upper Peninsula, along with accompanying economic hardship in the midst of declining demographics. The introduction of Canon 9, which allows for the ordination of indigenous priests and deacons in a given locale, was another important component, as were the people of the Upper Peninsula and the leaders they called forth, especially bishops Tom Ray and Jim Kelsey. The emergence of a thoroughly sacramental vision of creation and the eucharistic-centered ecclesiology of the Book of Common Prayer were other parts of the whole. There were certainly additional threads which added texture and subtle hue to this new church fabric, but these five were clearly present and essential.

We need to begin with the lakes and rivers that shape the land and the people of the Upper Peninsula. Cold and vast Lake Superior, the earth's largest body of fresh water, creates the northern shore of the peninsula, whereas the magnificent and distinct azure of Lake Michigan separates upper from lower Michigan. It was only in 1957 that the Mackinac suspension bridge was completed, uniting the two peninsulas. Until that time the choices were two: either take the ferry or fly.

Water not only virtually encompasses the Upper Peninsula, its rivers also course through the heavily forested interior, which used to be heavily mined. Michigan received the Upper Peninsula as a consolation prize after the bloodless battle with Ohio over the port of Toledo. Ohio received Toledo, and Michigan, along with its northern hinterland, was granted statehood in 1837. Years later its forests were coveted, especially after the Chicago fire, while rich veins of copper and iron ore drew miners to the Keweenaw peninsula and the central regions of the Upper Peninsula. Finns, Swedes, Cornish, and Italians were among the immigrants who came to fell lumber and extract ore during an all too brief economic boom. They did not necessarily mix well with one another, nor with the indigenous Ojibwa and Menomini peoples. Then came the bust. Boom and bust became the all too familiar economic cycle of this region.

It is helpful to bear in mind that the entire Upper Peninsula comprises about 16,538 square miles. At its widest, it runs three hundred ninety-four miles from west to east, and at its longest, two hundred thirty-three miles from north to south. This means that the peninsula constitutes roughly twenty-nine percent of Michigan's total geography, yet only three percent of the population resides here. It is larger in area than Massachusetts, Connecticut, Delaware, and Rhode Island combined, and exceeds the size of such countries as Belgium and Switzerland. Ninety percent of this land is covered by forest.

Out of the almost ten million people who inhabit Michigan, just over three hundred thousand live in the Upper Peninsula. In 1900, Houghton County had over sixty-six thousand residents; today that total stands at a little more than half. As recently as 1990, the Marquette County census was over seventy thousand, while today it is five thousand fewer. The copper is gone. A couple of iron mines struggle to function. Although the forest continues to be actively harvested for paper products, the Air Force base in Marquette closed ten years ago. Hospitals, schools, tourism, fill some of the labor gap, but not nearly enough. And the boom and bust cycle continues. All of this is simply to say that the Upper Peninsula is a rural and remote region with all of the accompanying economic challenges. Ironically, it is precisely its rural and remote character that has opened a door of possibility for the Episcopal Church here.

Canon 9

Canon 9 became part of Title III of the church's canons in 1970. We will discuss this canon later in the context of identifying some of the important issues raised by mutual ministry. For now, it is important to know, in the words of Rustin Kimsey, the retired Bishop of Eastern Oregon, that what made Canon 9 possible in the Episcopal Church were the apparent limitations placed on its use. It covers missionary opportunities in communities that are "small, isolated, remote, or distinct in respect of ethnic composition, language, or culture," and do not have regular access to sacramental and pastoral ministries. In such cases, the canon states,

> it shall be permissible for the Bishop, with the advice and consent of the Standing Committee . . . to establish procedures by which persons may be called by their Congregations and the Bishop with the Standing Committee, to be ordained local Priests and Deacons and licensed to serve the Congregations or communities out of which they were called.

The institution of Canon 9 offered a lifeline to such dioceses as Alaska, Nevada, and—come the mid-1980s—Northern Michigan. Dioceses, so long as they were sufficiently small and out of the way, or culturally and ethnically distinct, could identify, call forth, and form local residents for the presbyterate and diaconate.

The People

As we said above, only three percent of Michigan's approx-imately ten million women, men, and children live above the Mackinac bridge. Of those 300,000 or so, there are about 2,594 Episcopalians—a fraction of the Upper Peninsula's population, where Roman Catholics and Lutherans (ELCA, Missouri, Wisconsin, Apostolic) predominate.

Episcopalians have always been a small minority living in the villages and towns of the Upper Peninsula. Of the twenty-eight congregations in the diocese, only twenty-three remain open year-round. These figures have not changed all that much over the past twenty-five years.

It was just about twenty-five years ago that the diocese elected Tom Ray of Evanston, Illinois, to be its next bishop. He arrived to find a people of steely backbone and resolute character refined by persistently leaning into the harsh climate and eco-nomics of the region. This is a church which had survived against enormous odds—including the infamy of an early twentieth-century century bishop sent to prison for embezzling diocesan funds. This was also a church, despite all of the resolve it could muster, living on an economic precipice.

Most of the congregations had, and continue to have, fewer than seventy-five members for their average Sunday attendance. Additionally, businesses were leaving the area. Whereas between eighty and ninety percent of a congregation's disposable income could be directed toward outreach prior to 1950, the reality facing Tom Ray and the diocese was now starkly different. The same percentage of income that used to go for outreach now went to the vicar's salary. The reality was that stewardship and pledging had little or nothing to do with outreach and mission, but virtually everything with keeping the vicar afloat. Increasingly, the tempo-rary remedy was to cobble together a "cluster ministry" of small parishes sharing a single vicar, but that solution overlooked the ministerial gifts of parishioners themselves, exhausted the clergy, paid them miserably, and left the congregations still barely treading water.

Early into his episcopate, Tom brought in Jim Kelsey as a partner in ministry development. Slowly, deliberately, and not without mistakes and some pain along the way, the diocese began to weave a new vision, drawing bits of strength and purpose from the possibilities that lay about them. Within apparent scarcity, there was abundance. But, it would take some new eyes—some sacramental eyes—to see what was possible.

A Sacramental Vision

Tom Ray recognized, as he wrote later in an article for the *Anglican Theological Review*, that

> whenever we are troubled as Christians and Episcopalians, we return to the fundamentals. The spiritual taproot that we share as Christians and Episcopalians is the insight, the revelation and under-standing that this world our God has created is a sacra-mental world. That is why we have sacraments in the church, not because we are different or weird. We have a sacramental worship and spirituality because our world is sacramental.[2]

Because of the Episcopal Church's sacramental theology, he continues, it is not possible to divorce sacred from secular, temporal from eternal, the spiritual from the material. Yet Episcopalians have brought about

> a separation of ministry in the Church and ministry in the world. We have enshrined this separation in our national canons where clergy are responsible for spir-itual things and laity are responsible for temporal things. That, I believe, is bad sacramental theology.[3]

Prophetic voices speak all manner of messages, but all respond to the particular bondage that enslaves their own people.

Tom Ray's prophetic voice was born in part from his awareness that a good sacramental theology called the faithful communities of the Upper Peninsula into a new kind of church. His article articulates his discovery of fertile ground where he could nurture the continued growth, in breadth and depth, of a sacramental approach to creation, church, baptism, and ministry. Within this sacramental theology there would be no room for separation of sacred and secular. Or, put more positively, the sacramental world view would move our diocese forward toward the integration of all we are and do. Tom Ray's concern understandably remained focused primarily upon securing an administration of the sacraments for his own congregations, a pressing and legitimate need for the predominately rural diocese. Yet that by no means limits the relevance of this theology for the wider church; instead, sacramental theology is an invitation into a far-reaching reform of the whole church's way of life.

Tom Ray's article reflects the critical insight which he and others in the diocese came to fairly early on, that because of the separation between church and the world enshrined in our piety and canons of the church, clericalism and anti-clericalism was the result. The remedy? A church reformed by mutual ministry. This would be a church re-rooted in the faith that all of creation is of God and speaks of the glory of God. God's creation itself is holy, for it is of God, and to serve God in any place and in any way within this creation is to be in touch with God—it is to have a sacramental encounter.

From within this comprehensive sacramental proviso, the diocese initially restricted its focus to providing the sacraments to both financially limited and small, rural congregations. A sacramental people require real nourishment, and that can only occur through regular participation in the sacraments. For this regular participation to become a reality in small, rural, financially strapped congregations, it was necessary to remove the impediment caused by conventional understandings of calling and formation of the ordained ministries. With the identification and formation of individuals from within these congregations, on the other hand, it could become possible to provide for the regular celebration of the sacraments. This provision was not an end in itself, but was for the sake of providing support for the daily baptismal ministry of the members of the congregation. These ordained ministers were (and continue to be today) part of what Northern Michigan refers to as the Ministry Support Team. The Team would not minister to the congregation, but nurture and sustain it for ministry in the world.

A Eucharistic Ecclesiology

We have already begun to feel our way along this last thread that was essential to the weaving of mutual ministry in Northern Michigan. As Tom Ray traveled about the vast stretches of two-lane roads in the Upper Peninsula, moving from struggling congregation to struggling congregation, he began to ask himself and others in the words of the psalmist, how will we set a table in this wilderness?

According to the Book of Common Prayer, the celebration of the eucharist is presumed to be the primary and essential manner of Christian celebration of the day of resurrection. On the one hand, then, we had a church declaring that, as the people of God, we were called in and through our baptism to gather weekly around the altar-table, celebrating Christ's death, resurrection, and coming again in glory. Eucharist was not incidental to our life, nor was it an accessory brought into the church on special or rare occasions. Eucharist is, quintessentially, how we *are* church. And yet, on the other hand, we in Northern Michigan had been living with both a church tradition and economic realities that greatly hindered, if not outright prevented, such a eucharistic-centered life. Economically, we simply could no longer afford the conventional system of a seminary-trained cleric for each congregation. Ecclesiologically, we could no longer afford to have clergy-centered congregations. We needed to find a way to set the table, God's eucharistic table, within our wilderness if we were to know ourselves as the people we had been called to be through our baptism in the church.

How could our churches both survive and celebrate the eucharist? For us, celebration did not come after survival, but was the very means of survival! Our congregations were going under precisely because they continued to hang onto what they thought was their lifeline, but what was in reality the sinking weight of clericalism. If we were to survive in and through our celebration of the eucharist, our goal became clear: *we would have to transform our congregations from being communities gathered around a minister into ministering communities.* Tom Ray and Jim Kelsey sought out every opportunity—congregational meetings, Commission on Ministry meetings, Episcopal Church Women retreats, diocesan conventions—to engage the diocese in a conversation about this goal.

The diocese had taken into itself and inwardly digested the economic consumer model of our culture. Our congregations had been taught all too well that their lifeline was the rector or vicar who stood at the center of the congregation with the gifts necessary to lead the flock. Virtually all of the congregations' monies now went to support this vision of church and the more tightly they clung to it, the more certainly they all were sinking. They had inherited a consumer approach to church that created unhealthy and unholy dependency: under-subsidized clergy who had to be imported for the occasional eucharist. Within this consumerism came a marginalization of the God-given gifts resident in the baptized persons gathering each Sunday. This was not a way of life consistent with the church's eucharistic theology, nor was it economically sound. What was even more corrosive to the gospel, this system made church and eucharist dependent upon bad economics.

How would Northern Michigan set a table in the wilderness? Our churches could survive and celebrate the eucharist on a regular basis if we would journey together into mutual ministry. In the beginning, mutual ministry was our means for enabling our own small, rural, isolated, and financially strapped congregations to survive. Mutual ministry offered a way to identify, call forth, and form indigenous leadership. Mutual ministry was a way to ensure that any size community of baptized persons could set the eucharistic table in the wilderness. Through mutual ministry the Diocese of Northern Michigan began to transform congregations from being communities gathered around a minister into ministering communities.

But something unanticipated began to happen to us along the way.

---

[1] *The Gift: Poems by Hafiz the Great Sufi Master,* "Now is the Time," Daniel Ladinsky, Translator. (New York: Penguin Putnam, 1999), 160.

[2] Tom Ray, "The Small Church: Radical Reformation and Renewal of Ministry," *Anglican Theological Review* (Vol. LXXX, No. 4, Fall 1998), 617.

[3] Ibid., 618.

༄

CHAPTER SIX

The Strength of That Center

Psalm 22

Do not be far from me
Be the center
Of the center
Of the circle
Be the strength of that center[1]

In the beginning, mutual ministry was about survival. "Success" would depend upon our ability to appropriately weave together each of the vital threads into the fabric of a new common life—the goal was ministering communities. A ministering community is a congregation that has identified, called forth, and developed the gifts of its baptized members. As we began to live into this journey gradually, over the course of two decades, the focus of our ministry development became less about survival and more about life transformation.

The Italian painter Giorgio de Chirico has a magnificent piece entitled "Nostalgia," which depicts two excruciatingly small figures standing isolated and very insignificant before an immense tower. It is a picture of isolation and longing. The tower and shadows of the picture dwarf the barely human figures—people who long for something more.

In western culture, our lives live and breathe duality: light and dark, good and evil, heaven and hell, sacred and profane.

It is almost as if we have bifocal vision in our very genes, so that "separate and divide" is the default setting of the human exercise of judgment. Our search and our nostalgia is for a re-membering of our fractured world. We hunger to glue the pieces back together again. Humpty-Dumpty is less a child's fairy tale than it is the nightmare of day-to-day existence.

And yet, the sacramental vision guiding the development of mutual ministry in the Upper Peninsula presupposes an entirely different picture. So the problem is not with the way things actually are, but with how we have been taught to see. As the mystics of both East and West remind us again and again, we do not see reality the way it is, but the way we have been taught to see it. And, contrary to our own sacramental theology, we have all too often assumed that fracture, not wholeness, underlies creation and society. But the first and final Word is wholeness, not division. When we proclaim in the Prayer Book collect that in God we live, move, and have our being, this is no rhetorical flourish—this is the marrow of our faith. What we long for is to taste once again, in the words of mystic Richard Rohr, that literally, "everything belongs."

We of the Diocese of Northern Michigan have begun to wake up to the reality that God is in everything—a sacramental vision of life claims nothing less. Mutual ministry is rooted in the conviction that every single person, created in the image and likeness of God, is gifted to serve. Mutual ministry thus begins to move us beyond the separations that have lingered within our vision, such as sacred and secular, natural and supernatural. If all creation is a sacrament, then all reveals the presence of God if we have but eyes to see. As the hymn reminds us, "in Christ there is no East or West, in Christ no North or South." Or, as Meister Eckhart experienced in his life—in the end, all there is, is God. For us, mutual ministry became a kind of solvent, slowly yet surely dissolving the false line fracturing the vision of ourselves and creation. In the words of Psalm 33, we began to glimpse the truth behind the declaration that "the earth is *full* of your kindness, the heavens are *made* of your word."[2]

Mutual ministry, we began to see, was not simply a means of survival made possible by the introduction of Canon 9, but a way of awakening us to an entirely different way of being the people of God. We, in the isolated and rural hinterland, through our hunger for survival in the wilderness, had stumbled upon a "saving" realization: God was always, already with us. Now was the season to know, in the words of the mystic Hafiz with which this part of the book began, that "everything you do is sacred." In each and every thing, God is always already *wholly* present.

A God wholly present in every nook and cranny of creation, in every person, is the implication of the sacramental theology spoken by Tom Ray. The body of Christ is indeed the church, but it is much, much, more—creation is the very body of Christ. Baptism is to be the water washing away all divisions in our vision and way of life. Eucharist reminds us that each and every table around which we gather is a feeding by God of God's own. Our mission as the people of God is to be a witness that this is so—everyone belongs to and is fed by God. Everyone belongs and is called forth to be a minister of God. We are no longer consumer "communities" in a secular culture of consumption, but ministering communities in a thoroughly sacred creation.

And yet, we in Northern Michigan, along with everyone else in the United States, live and breathe a culture of "rugged individualism." We are taught to try and stand alone like the figures in de Chirico's painting. We nostalgically long for something more, but are taught that such longing is a sign of weakness and a character flaw. The result of such rugged individualism is what is known as the post-modern fragmented life—no common purpose, no common story, no underlying unity.

Mutual ministry invites us to know ourselves in a fundamentally different and transformative way. We are not lone rangers.

We are not isolated. We are one—distinct, to be sure, but fully one. But so often we cannot see how this is so. As our diocese's journey into mutual ministry continued, we began to see much more clearly that it was not enough to teach people about an alternative sacramental vision of life. In the early days of mutual ministry, we had developed a curriculum for use in our congregations to help educate and develop the Covenant Groups that were eventually commissioned as the Ministry Support Teams, which nurtured the ministry of all baptized persons. But this curriculum no longer satisfied us. We needed a process, the very nature of which would be to continually dissolve the walls of separation, helping us to rediscover the union of prayer, work, spirituality, study, play, and worship. In other words, we needed a process to help us taste our commonality, our unity, our common story, with one another in Christ. We were also aware that others had been on their own journeys into mutual (or total) ministry, and perhaps now was the appropriate time to draw upon one another's wisdom and create a new process for ongoing, or life-long, formation in community.

LifeCycles

For almost twenty years our diocese supported congregations as they identified, called forth, and formed members of the faith community to take full responsibility for their own ministry. This support was based on the diocese's belief that every congregation is endowed by the Spirit with all the gifts necessary to flourish. Those called came to form a Covenant Group: collaborating to nurture and develop the ministry of all baptized members of the congregation. After a time of preparation, the entire group was commissioned (and those called to the presbyterate and diaconate, ordained) as the Ministry Support Team in the context of a Celebration of Baptismal Ministry of the entire congregation. A team might have anywhere between five and twenty members, including preachers, deacons, presbyters, and coordinators for diaconal ministry, worship, stewardship, ecumenism, and catechesis.

People from across the country and around the world were drawn to the simplicity of the process and its ability to empower the baptized and to renew local congregations. The diocese developed special Visitors Weekends to help accommodate the constant stream of people seeking to explore the face of mutual ministry in the Upper Peninsula. These weekends provided an opportunity for a "mini-immersion" into our experience of mutual ministry.

By the late 1990s, the original curriculum guiding the formation of the Ministry Support Teams was beginning to show signs of age, and the diocese realized that the time had come to revise it. After several years of work within the diocese, developmental partners were invited to join the writing team, bringing a wealth of experience from many quarters. The Diocese of Nevada had years of experience in local ministry development, begun during the episcopacy of Wesley Frensdorff. The Diocese of Wyoming was doing innovative work in ministry development in the isolated congregations dotting the state, and both were active participants in a national movement in ministry development known as "Living Stones." Within New England, an organization called "Harvesters" was also attempting to break new ground in mutual ministry, linking up dioceses with the efforts of the regional seminaries.

In sum, *LifeCycles* was born of the collaborative effort of the dioceses of Northern Michigan, Nevada, Wyoming, the seven dioceses of New England through the Harvesters Partnership, and an organization called LeaderResources.[3] What began as a way for Northern Michigan to update its ministry development curriculum was itself transformed into the offering of a Christian formation process for the whole church, shaped by a thoroughly sacramental vision of life.

LifeCycles is not a curriculum. It is a process of formation, or more accurately, transformation in the context of community.

LifeCycles is a formation process suitable for any community, which is to say any group of people willing to come together on a regular basis to explore what it means to trust in a God who is always already present. *LifeCycles* is an ongoing process of Christian transformation in community which embodies radical commitment to gospel mutuality. The very structure of *LifeCycles* is one way it forms its participants in a community whose guiding values are those of mutual creativity, love, liberty, and restorative justice—reflective of the triune God who is at once Creator, Lover, and Liberator.

For *LifeCycles* to do what it is intended to do, we had to embody and nurture the sacramental vision articulated twenty years earlier by Tom Ray. *LifeCycles* could not be a linear cur-riculum—that is, a course of study that progresses from a set beginning to a set end. Rather, it needed to be a process of for-mation in community and in the midst of life. We needed some-thing akin to a new spiritual DNA, from which our communities could continually draw as a guide to becoming every more fully aware of the thorough sacredness of all that is.

Gordon Lathrop, in his marvelous books, *Holy Things* and *Holy People*, proved to be a vital inspiration to the development of the *LifeCycles* foundational statement. One of the insights of Lathrop's liturgical theology is that there are some very simple, deceptively simple, things that Christians do. We are creatures who gather together. We tell stories that remind us who we are, as well as what we value and fear. We are fascinated by water—drawn inexorably to it while knowing equally well it has the power to drown us. We also cannot seem to help but gather around food—we are creatures of community meal. What our Christianity does is provide a context of meaning for all of these human activities. Most importantly, as Christians we gather, tell stories, play with water, share a meal, and go forth, within the context of celebrating and serving the reign of God.

Much of the beauty and power of Lathrop's liturgical theology, I believe, is what I would describe as its cross-cultural validity. In other words, everyone gathers, tells stories, plays with water, shares a meal, and goes forth. What do these things mean? That depends on the person and culture. But the actions bespeak an underlying commonality as human creatures of the living God. Life is about becoming aware of the meaning these actions have for us. Or to put it slightly differently, life is about becoming aware of how God (however we "know" God) is continually disclosed in and through these utterly ordinary activities of daily life. *LifeCycles* thus developed its foundational statement:

We are a community gathered and sent forth by the Spirit
To encounter our story,
To be washed and renewed,
To be fed with thanksgiving, and
To celebrate and serve the reign of God.

This statement expresses the spiritual DNA of *LifeCycles*. Christian transformation in community transpires in a spiraling journey, continually touching base with these essential building blocks of our life in Christ. Each clause of the statement describes a unit of formation (e.g., Gathered by the Spirit, Sent Forth by the Spirit, Encountering our Story), which group members consider through the lenses of experience, creativity, love, liberty, and restorative justice. Each journey through the *LifeCycles* spiral also brings participants into conversation with the Hebrew and Christian scriptures, as well as the voices of history (that is, the lives of the saints).

The actual session format of *LifeCycles* again reflects the basic things we as human beings do. In other words, *LifeCycles* is itself formation through liturgy. Humans are by nature liturgical beings for whom the eucharist is not a foreign imposition. We gather to set the table and hear stories and immerse in water because these most basic human actions remind us that God is found in the most ordinary acts of life. Eucharistic liturgy is how human beings live. Each and every culture has its way of giving thanks (offering eucharist) for the utter giftedness of life. The eucharist is sacred because every eucharist—every gathering, every table, every story, every bath and every sip of water, every sending—is sacred. God is either everywhere or nowhere. This is the truth we long to know in our heart of hearts. We long to know it not in our heads, as some fact we memorize, but as something we personally taste and which has the power to guide us in life and through death.

Something has been happening to the people of Northern Michigan during their journey into mutual ministry. Tom Ray, Jim Kelsey, and the baptized persons of Northern Michigan are helping us all to discover that a sacramental vision of community life is the Spirit's invitation to the entire church to learn to listen again for the voices of the gifted around us.

The gifts that the church is listening for, first of all, are those that speak to us from the fields of their labor in God's sacred creation—the sacrament undergirding the church and all other sacraments. The starting place for mutual ministry, for the ministry of all baptized persons, is the sacrament of God's creation in which we live, move, and have our being. I do not know how we can support, or be supported by, those whom we do not know and explicitly fail to include in the formation of our own faith and ministry. Christian formation, by its very nature, yearns to be inclusive—a sacramental vision requires no less. As a consequence, mutuality grows from common experience, common life, common prayer, and common hope. In other words, it grows from friendship—"I do not call you servants any longer, because the servant does not know what the master is doing; but I have called you friends. . ." (John 15:15).

We would do a great disservice to the thought of Tom Ray, and the mutual ministry it continues to nurture within the church, if we were to understand it essentially as a means, albeit valid and worthy, for small and rural churches throughout our communion to sustain a life nurtured by the sacraments. *It is this and so very much more.* As Rustin Kimsey, former Bishop of Eastern Oregon, proclaims, the challenge mutual ministry lays before us is one of reformation that is at least as profound as that of the sixteenth century. These are bold words, yet, I believe true. We cannot allow mutual ministry, which is simply a shorthand way for expressing the faith-in-action of the baptismal covenant, to be dismissed (even unintentionally) as a survival package for weak and isolated congregations. The kind of mutual ministry pioneered in such places as Northern Michigan, Wyoming, and Nevada, as well as in dioceses of Canada and New Zealand, like the inaugural act of Jesus' ministry, begins by proclaiming the year of the Lord's favor on all those whom we have allowed to survive by whatever means possible (Luke 4:19). The Spirit is now inviting the church to appreciate the rural and small congregation as the threshold to a reformed and thoroughly sacramental church. Mutual ministry is teaching us all anew how to set an overflowing table, provided that the church is willing to listen to and wrestle with the questions raised by the crossing of this sacramental threshold.

---

[1] Norman Fischer, *Opening to You: Zen-Inspired Translations of the Psalms* (New York: Penguin Putnam, 2002), 32.

[2] Ibid., 51 (emphasis added).

[3] It is possible to review *LifeCycles* by visiting the website of LeaderResources at www.leaderresources.org.

✦
CHAPTER SEVEN

Leadership and the Gifts of Ministry

As we begin to re-root formation and ministry within the baptismal covenant, new issues arise. They are quite practical in nature, each carrying in its wake significant implications for our way of being church. To quote liturgical scholar Ruth Myers, what is transpiring is nothing less than the development of a baptismally grounded church. In her book, *Continuing the Reformation: Re-visioning Baptism in the Episcopal Church*, she writes:

> I believe that the twentieth-century revolution in baptismal practice and theology in the Episcopal Church is bringing about a baptismal ecclesiology, an understanding of the Church as a community formed by baptism and empowered by baptism and the eucharist to carry out the reconciling ministry of Christ in the world.[1]

As the journey toward a baptismally grounded church continues, new issues and challenges will inevitably surface. But for now I want to focus on four questions, which will be the subject of this and the following chapter:

First, who is going to help a congregation journey from being a religious "consumer group" to a community that is rooted in the ministry of all the baptized?

Second, each and every congregation, regardless of size or financial wealth, needs to ask itself: What are the gifts the Spirit has endowed us with? How do we nurture these gifts and give them the broad space of freedom to flourish?

Third, if it is true that mutual ministry is inviting us into a more fully reformed way of life, how will we encourage a universal acceptance of the ministries identified, called forth, and formed, regardless of the locale?

Fourth, what are to be the church's expectations of those identified, called, and formed, prior to ordination and commissioning? To what degree need someone be equipped before being blessed, if you will, to exercise his or her gift as ministry on behalf of and in the name of the church?

To begin with the first question, the traditional role of a rector who has been educated and formed at seminary seems particularly ill suited to the task of helping a community become one that is rooted in the ministry of all the baptized. There seems to be a divide between the conventional expectations of a rector and the midwifery of community gifts and ministry that is called for in the baptismally grounded church of mutual ministry. Since clericalism inhibits a thorough baptismal reformation of our community life, mutual ministry depends upon surmounting, or better, dissolving, this divide. Practically speaking it requires both the reintegration of clerical leadership within the body of the baptized and the subsequent exercise of baptismal leadership in a manner consistent with the gospel command for mutuality between members of the body. I believe that the role of "ministry developer," which includes persistent inviting, midwifing, and mentoring, has the capacity to fulfill both these needs.[2] Here, I want to concentrate on continuing to plumb the implications of Tom Ray's sacramental theology, discussed earlier, for our way of life. I think they go to the heart of the place and role of leadership. We begin with the reintegration of leadership within community life.

If we are all created in the image of God, and through baptism made full members in the body of Christ, then ordination can no longer be enshrined in canon and ministry as a sacramental divide rendering class separation—clerical and lay—within the church. Our primary sense of identity has to flow from the common waters of our baptism in Christ. As the Lutheran theologian Jürgen Moltmann says so eloquently in his book, *The Spirit of Life: A Universal Affirmation*, the Christian life is about rebirth into freedom. We cannot be free within a sacramentally and canonically sanctioned class system. What we are about, Jürgen Moltmann proclaims, is "Life in the Spirit [as] a life in the 'broad place where there is no cramping' (Job 36:16)."[3]

The leadership role of the traditional rector is the product of an unacceptable power structure that perpetuates the deep divide of clergy and lay. This division results in the false elevation of clergy and the consequent devaluing of laity ("I'm just a lay person"). Moltmann provides a stinging critique of this kind of hierarchy that results from the "over-extension of the head-body image for the Church," which only serves to perpetuate division. In the church's "true unity," Moltmann writes, it reflects the unity within the Trinity, whose persons

> express the community by expressing themselves,
> and—conversely—the community gives expression to
> the persons by giving expression to itself. In this
> complementarity there is no priority.[4]

Thus we need to re-envision leadership within a "fellowship of equals," rather than as a sole, ordained individual who is licensed to act as the dominating head and ruler of the body. It is quite likely that we need a new name, or renewed name, to convey the manner of leadership exercised by those in fellowship with their sisters and brothers in Christ. What we are searching for, in part, is an understanding of leadership capable of helping our own clergy re-imagine their place and role within their community. Many of the ordained yearn to shed the encumbrances of rule and primacy associated with rectorship, but do not know how or where to begin.

In *Engaging the Powers,* biblical scholar Walter Wink uses archaeological evidence to show that "partnership societies" may have existed in prehistoric times, which functioned by means of cooperation and were characterized by "actualization hierarchies (where leaders serve the community) rather than domination hierarchies (where communities must serve the leaders)."[5] Indeed, during the first century, at the heart of the good news preached by Jesus, is the counter-cultural declaration that we are his friends and not servants (John 15:15). Or, as Paul proclaims in Galatians 3:28, in Christ "There is no longer Jew or Greek, there is no longer slave or free, there is no longer male and female; for all of you are one in Christ Jesus."

I am not proposing that there once existed a golden age of utter equality, nor do I believe in a pristine and primitive Christian egalitarianism that it is our goal to resurrect. But traces of an alternative way of life are often present in history if we know where to look, and these traces can reveal attempts at more equitably based community relations and leadership. The Spirit does not invite us to resurrect the past, but calls out to us to be co-creators of a future that has yet to be. Equality and mutuality are reservoirs for gospel-based hope—deep pools from which our spirits draw strength to continue the endless struggle for reformation. These values are signposts, guiding us in the focus of our gaze into history so that we might learn from those who have sacrificed all for this hope.

I believe that Moltmann's and Wink's critique of domination hierarchies applies to the kind of leadership that the church still experiences today. Is it possible that the Spirit is at play among us, inviting us to learn how, as leaders, to live out a "power with" the communities in which we live, move, and have our being, the communities of our friends in Christ? I have been arguing for just this possibility, claiming that the gospels call us into a community of equals. Indeed, equality lies at the liberating heart of Jesus' good news. This community of equals is basically consistent with the concept of actualization hierarchy (which we have also called holarchy) in which partnership, not domination, characterizes interaction within the community.

The movement I propose from "rector" to "ministry developer," therefore, entails doing much more than a change of name. It signifies transforming the expectations we have of each other, expectations that reflect the kind of relationship in which we understand ourselves to be participants. We are in search of a form of leadership that reflects a living and breathing commitment to partnership, reintegrating our leaders within the common life of the baptized.

In referring to a leader as a ministry developer, I am not speaking exclusively of the role being carried out by the seminary-trained missioners (most of whom are still presbyters) within dioceses such as Northern Michigan and Wyoming. These are two of the many dioceses that already live into some form of the ministry of all the baptized. In such dioceses the missioner shares (with the local leaders, the other missioners, and the bishop) in the oversight of a number of congregations, whereas the rector/vicar retains a place of primacy within a particular congregation. I am suggesting that the vocation of ministry developer can provide a theologically and scripturally sounder understanding of oversight ministry than that of rector or vicar, without the baggage of the somewhat anachronistic language of rector/vicar. To speak of ministry development offers the chance to reconceive the role of oversight consistent with the vision of community articulated in the baptismal covenant. (It may well be that in this process of re-conception, we will cease to use the term "oversight," with its parental overtones.) To state this paradoxically, a ministry developer's work consists in undergirding a community of partnership and complementarity.

Persistent Inviter

Once we have begun to reintegrate congregational leadership within the body of Christ, how will the ministry developer lead? How will the necessary oversight and undergirding transpire? If the Spirit's wisdom dwells within the body of Christ, I believe we would do well to conceive the ministry developer's relationship with the body as that of a midwife who *persistently invites*. The way of the Spirit is not to manipulate, control, or dominate. Accordingly, the ministry developer leads by inviting the community to consider the various thresholds of possibility that lie before it. This is not an invitation to be passive, nor is it invitation to consider possibilities without asking for guidance. The ministry developer's responsibility is to help the community (whether a region or a single congregation) consider possibilities in the light of the baptismal covenant.

As the *persistent inviter*, the decision about which threshold to cross (for example, in matters of worship, outreach, stewardship) is not the ministry developer's alone to make. A consensus is to be sought, reached through the community's shared wisdom of discernment under the spiritual guidance of the ministry developer. The ministry developer midwifes the discernment process, but without seizing control of it, manipulating it, or undermining it. This is especially important when the ministry developer's own sense of wisdom may not be in agreement with that of the community. Let me draw on some wise words from Mary Benet McKinney, OSB, from her book entitled *Sharing Wisdom: A Process for Group Decision Making*. God is inviting the ministry developer into what McKinney describes as a kind of "holy indifference." It is the ability

> to "let go" and seek the will of the Spirit in the gathered wisdom rather than in the wisdom of any one individual. . . . Just as none of us can be church alone, so none of us can hear the total wisdom of the Spirit

alone. We need each other; we need to surrender to the
God of the Gathering.

This holy indifference, the ability to let go of my piece of the wisdom, is crucial to the life of the ministry of all the baptized.
Without this habit of the heart, the ministry developer, in times of
conflict and disagreement, will easily be drawn back into becoming
the ruler and arbiter, attempting to reduce the adults to the role of
disciplined children. McKinney is quite frank about the reality of
community life and its tensions. It is possible, she writes,

> that an individual member of the group will not be
> able to accept a decision. When this happens, neither
> that person nor the group should feel that this inability
> to surrender to the wisdom of the group represents a
> failure to discern.... But there is also a time to let go
> of the ideal and live with the reality. Discernment is
> neither miraculous nor magical. It is a call to simplicity
> of heart, a willingness to struggle through the journey
> within the human limitations to be found in one's self
> and in one another.

And why is the ministry developer willing to struggle through
this journey, when personal surrender to the group's wisdom is
elusive at best? From trust in the wider workings of the Spirit,
and from the recognition that "a discerned decision [is not] to be
seen as final and forever. Life is a dynamic reality. Situations and
people and needs change."[6]

Midwife

The ministry developer is one who midwifes the congregation through a birth of awareness of the presence of guiding
Wisdom within the body of Christ. The ministry developer is not
the head of the body or the brains of the outfit. The ministry
developer is not the gifted wonder-worker or the arbiter of
Robert's Rules of Order. The ministry developer is a member of
the body who acts persistently to invite communal and personal

consideration of how the Spirit is gifting us now and calling us to praise God and serve creation. Convinced of the giftedness of the body of Christ, a ministry developer knows that within any and every congregation are people gifted for serving God in creation, as well as people who are gifted to lead the community of faith in worship.

Mentor

Another way of describing the image of midwifery as a part of ministry development leadership is to draw on that of mentoring. The mentor, above all, is one who knows the communities with whom she works. Knowing implies the development of a relationship of deep trust. It is this relationship that enables the mentor to discern where the community is in its own discernment and formation process. The mentor is the companion, what Celtic spirituality might describe as an *anamchara*, to the community.

Relational responsibility characterizes these interactions with the community, by which I mean that the mentor develops relationships through the experiences of daily life in order to be able to respond appropriately to the movement of the Spirit within the community. The ministry developer will be someone who shares in the community's encounters with the Spirit of God through dialogue with the lectionary scriptures. The ministry developer joins in the exploration of the baptismal covenant. These experiences, and the relationships that develop through them, enable the ministry developer to help give birth to gifts, discernment, and exploration of the baptismal covenant in the years to come.

From Needs to Gifts

If, like the disciple Paul, we are convinced of the giftedness of the body of Christ, and believe that within any and every congregation are people equipped to serve God in creation as in worship, then the church would be wise to root ministry development in the gifts that are present in a particular community.

It is not unusual to hear from those in larger and wealthier congregations objecting to the ministry of all the baptized, on the grounds that their congregation has no need for it:

> We already have the priest we need in our rector. We've called her and pay her amply for the services she delivers. Let those in need—the poorer and smaller congregations—call forth members from their communities to be presbyters and deacons on their behalf. They have a right to receive the sacraments and this arrangement meets their legitimate, special, needs. But we already have "our" priest and have no need for others. Besides, what do we pay her for?

Such an attitude has missed the point of community life in the Spirit. Search the Christian scriptures as we will, we will not discover a theology of ministry based primarily upon need. Needs are important, but they are not the basis upon which Christian ministry is founded. A needs-based approach to ministry is attractive, however, because it gives us a sense of control, even if illusory, of the body of Christ. We determine our needs and respond to them. Ministry, in this case, begins with us. A needs-based approach also feels right, for we live in a therapeutic culture that has its starting point in the particular needs of a person or group.

St. Paul takes a different tack, however. From Paul's writing, as well as from the scriptures as a whole, it is quite clear that our response to the Spirit's presence within and about us is that of thankfulness for gifts given. We will not find the early Christian movement, as it is portrayed in the Christian scriptures, endeavoring to limit ministry to a series of responses to perceived needs. The starting point is the gifts given. In other words, for each and every congregation the questions to consider, regardless of size and financial wealth, are, "What are the gifts the Spirit has endowed us with? How do we nurture these gifts and give them the broad space of freedom to flourish?"

From the beginning, creation and all its wonders have been and continue to be a gift from the Creator. The church is called to respond with thanksgiving for what lies before us and within us, and then, invited by the Spirit, to nurture these gifts in Christian ministry. In short, ministry begins with God and God's gifts, not with our needs and us. To begin ministry with gifts given asks that we trust in God's often chaotically creative ways.

Theologian and missionary Roland Allen was fond of saying a basic truth about Christian community life: all the gifts are there to flourish. When any congregation fails to recognize, respect, and nurture these gifts, it squanders the profligate abundance of God. This is true for both gifts of service to creation and in worship. Every congregation has people within it gifted by the Spirit to gather people around God's table and be a reconciling presence in their midst. Every congregation has people within it gifted by the Spirit to proclaim the word and send the people forth emboldened to serve in God's world. Every congregation has people within it gifted by the Spirit to speak publicly of their faith and the scriptures in a way meaningful for their community. Every congregation has people within it gifted by the Spirit to care compassionately for one another, listening well without offering false and facile solutions to genuine pain, suffering, and struggle. Such gifts, respectively, embody the ministries for the presbyterate, diaconate, preaching, and pastoral care.

The ministry developer who, as midwife, inviter, and mentor, works in concert with the bishop and Commission on Ministry to help the community identify these gifts within its midst, also helps to develop and form them through education and prayer as they are exercised on behalf of the community. This ministry developer's work differs from that of a rector or vicar, who, in an effort to justify both presence and salary, may feel obliged to assume control of every ministry in the parish.

The church is in error whenever it insists that a congregation has no need to identify those in its midst with the gifts for such ministries as worship, diaconal ministry, preaching, and pastoral care. If local formation for ministry is understood as based on need, then the church acts in the manner of noblesse oblige—it offers local formation as a rescue parachute. If, however, we begin with the reality of God's profligate generosity, then the church is responding in deep gratitude for the gifts given. The church is there to harvest what God has wonderfully sown.

The gifts are there if we have the courage to look. Courage, because we must be willing to allow the Spirit to guide the community into a new way of being the faithful of Jesus. We must trust that if we attend to, nurture, and provide the broad space of freedom for the gifts to flourish, the Spirit will indeed guide us into new ways of life and mission.

---

[1] Ruth A. Myers, *Continuing the Reformation: Re-visioning Baptism in the Episcopal Church* (New York: Church Publishing Incorporated, 1997), xvi.

[2] I am indebted to Phina Borgeson and Lynne Wilson for this insight into the use of "ministry developer." I encourage the reader to visit the website for the Ministry Developers Collaborative at www.mindevelopers.org.

[3] Jürgen Moltmann, *The Spirit of Life: A Universal Affirmation* (Minneapolis: Fortress Press, 1994), 178.

[4] Ibid., 224.

[5] Wink, *Engaging the Powers,* 37.

[6] Mary Benet McKinney, OSB., *Sharing Wisdom: A Process for Group Decision Making* (Allen, Texas: Tabor Publishing, 1987), 17; 161-62.

✤
CHAPTER EIGHT

"Local": The Place of Call, Formation, and Service

One of the issues that our continuing journey into mutual ministry has begun to raise for us repeatedly is our understanding of the term "local." The baptismally grounded church of mutual ministry is inviting us into a more catholic way of life. Within our communion there needs to be a universal acceptance of the baptismal ministries that have been identified, called forth, and formed. Without this universal acceptance, the church runs the risk of disintegrating into a much more fragmented way of life. But there is an apparent stumbling block to full acceptance of baptismal ministries and this is the meaning of the term "local" in our canons. It is necessary, therefore, for us to reconsider the theology of local within Title III, Canon 9.[1]

Section 1 (a), states:

> With regard to Dioceses with Congregations or missionary opportunities in communities which are small, isolated, remote, or distinct in respect of ethnic composition, language, or culture, and which cannot be provided sufficiently with the sacraments and pastoral ministrations of the Church through Clergy ordained under the provisions of Canon III.7, it shall be permissible for the Bishop, with the advice and consent of the Standing Committee . . . . to establish procedures by which persons may be called by their

Congregations and the Bishop with the Standing
Committee, to be ordained local Priests and Deacons
and licensed to serve the Congregations or communities
out of which they were called.

Small, Isolated, Remote

Canon 9 raises a host of issues. Let's try to grapple with
them as they arise. The first issue which this section seeks to
address and redress is the lack of the "sacraments and pastoral
ministrations" within a congregation due to its being "small, isolated,
remote, or distinct in respect of ethnic composition, language or
culture." As we discussed above, this is a legitimate concern to
which Tom Ray of Northern Michigan has spoken at some length.
The problem for us, however, is that the present canonical remedy,
in the long run, is worse than the affliction. The underlying issue
is not one essentially of ministration of sacraments and pastoral
care. Rather, it is what kind of church are we to be and how are
we to carry out the ministries reflective of the gifts given by the
Spirit to this kind of church?

Pivotal to our reformed and catholic understanding of the
church is our theology of the Spirit, which affirms that *gifts
bestowed to the people of any particular locale are not contingent
upon that locale being "small, isolated, remote, or distinct in
respect of ethnic composition, language, or culture."* The Spirit
blows where the Spirit will. The gifts for the presbyterate and the
diaconate are present within any community regardless of size,
location, ethnicity, language, or culture. They are present, along
with many other gifts, because the people of God, the body of
Christ, is there and alive. The challenge before us is not one of
artificially limiting the possible conditions that allow for the
presence of gifts for ministry, but of developing formation
processes appropriate to the conditions in which we find God's
Spirit moving and inviting God's people forth.

Licensed to Serve

A second and related issue arising from this section of Canon 9 concerns the clause stating that the "local Priests and Deacons . . . [are] licensed to serve the Congregations out of which they were called." Broadly speaking, I would think that it is true of any presbyter and deacon that, before they are licensed to exercise their ministries, it must be clear that a community has called them forth to serve. Since we are part of a communion, with the diocese embodying, preserving, and promoting our unity, it is in fact the diocese itself that requests the service of the locally formed presbyter and deacon. Admittedly, I am clearly expanding the meaning of "call" in this canon. But whether someone receives formation locally or within a seminary of the Episcopal Church, it ought to be the normal expectation that before beginning to serve in an official capacity, the ordinand's presence is first recognized and affirmed by the community and its leadership. If this were the understanding behind licensing, then the requirement for licensing would cease to be contingent upon the location of the formation process.

Rooted in the Community

A third issue concerns one of the qualifications of ordinands stipulated in Canon 9, Section 1 (b) (3). The canon states that they "shall be recognized as leaders in the Congregation and shall be firmly rooted in the community." This qualification should be true, in differing ways, for all those called to be presbyters and deacons. Whether an individual's formation process has occurred locally or within a seminary, responsible leadership that will be embraced by the congregation will only transpire if the leaders are "recognized" and "firmly rooted in the community." Rootedness is simply a form of shorthand, for ministry always occurs within the context of actual relationships. All authentic leadership, therefore, is rooted in a ministering community—ministers are not lone rangers.

One of the challenges that the current situation created by Canon 9 presents to traditional parish ministry is the fact that the recognition of clergy is initially rooted not in the community of brothers and sisters of which they are to be part, but in the institutional church hierarchy. Here we must distinguish between knowledge and power on the one hand, and Christian leadership on the other. Seminary training and ordination bestow power, but servant leadership will only develop from building relationships with the people, which is simply a long way of saying that one has become rooted in the community's life. In sum, it is not a matter of some ordained servants being firmly rooted and others not. All authentic leadership is rooted leadership. Ironically, precisely because the seminary formation process separates the person from both the community that has called him forth and the community that will call him to service, the rooting process is bound to take longer. On the other hand, those who are locally identified, called forth, and formed are already an essential part of their community.

The matter of rootedness leads us to another issue. We do not need to understand rooted to mean congregationally restricted. This is important because Sections 7 and 8 of Canon 9 seek to place limitations of movement on the locally called and formed presbyters and deacons. Let us look at each section in turn.

Section 7 states that "If Deacons or Priests who have been ordained in accordance with this Canon shall subsequently remove to another community within the Diocese, they shall be entitled to exercise their office in that place only if: (a) Requested by the Congregation; and (b) The Bishop licenses them." The vision of church shaping Section 7 is catholic, and not congregationalist, if we understand it to say that presbyters and deacons, recognized by the full communion as legitimately and validly ordained ministers, must be invited by a congregation and licensed by the bishop before they can serve on behalf of the congregation and diocese. But such an understanding of church life, once again, ought not to be circumscribed to fit only those whose original calling and formation was local. Should not the stipulations of Section 7 be universally applicable? If a presbyter's or deacon's presence has not been requested by a congregation, what on earth is she doing there? Would it not also be true that once called and formed, a "local" presbyter and deacon could be requested by congregations within a region of the diocese, or by the diocese as a whole, to be available for service wherever needed? As far as the matter of how the licensing transpires, this is a process best left to the discretion of the bishop and the Diocesan Commission on Ministry.

When we turn to Section 8 of Canon 9, we read, "It is the normal expectation that persons ordained under the provisions of this Canon shall not move from the Congregation and Diocese in which they were ordained." As far as this provision is concerned, I find neither ecclesiological justification nor cultural basis. If the church has affirmed that the persons identified, called forth, formed, and ordained, as presbyters and deacons are properly formed and duly ordained throughout the whole church, then they are here to serve where congregations and dioceses of the church request and license their service. Even within the most rural regions of Nevada, Wyoming, and Northern Michigan, people move in and out of congregations. By and large, ours is a thoroughly mobile society. It is the common expectation that most of us will indeed move, and that includes persons currently ordained under the provisions of Canon 9.

Perhaps it is true to say that Section 8 provides a sense of security for those who are unsure of the wisdom of local call and formation. In this case it can be seen as supplying a tether, preventing the unleashing of Canon 9 upon the rest of the church. Yet it must also be said that it perpetuates separate and unequal presbyterates and diaconates in the church, and flies in the face of social realities.

A Theology of the Local

If we are to be consistent with the wisdom of our baptismally grounded church, we must come to honor those who are locally called and formed as ministers whose ministry is catholic—that is, recognized as valid and legitimate throughout the Anglican Communion. Instead, the church has traditionally held up one primary means of forming presbyters and deacons, along with some latitude for adaptation, as a necessary condition for catholic recognition of orders throughout the whole church. It is undeniable that economic issues—especially pension and insurance—are part of this proposal to recognize the catholicity of those who are locally called, formed, and ordained; but economics should not dictate sound theology and way of life. Rather, sound theology and ecclesiology invite us to rework our economic structure so that it can support the gifts for ministry with which the Spirit has endowed us.

Our canons need to be reformed so as to reflect a "theology of the local" as referring to place of origin, formation, and service. In other words, some presbyters and deacons, along with other ministries, will be identified, called forth, formed, and serve from within their local congregation or region. This given community of faith and its mission in the world will define the parameters of their primary ministry. But as a specific and particular embodiment of the church catholic, the local church calls on behalf of the church catholic for service of its people. If this is not the case, then we are engaging in congregationalist practices without admitting it.

A presbyter who gathers people around the table and reconciles them is engaging in actions with universal, or catholic, meaning in the Anglican Communion. Without doubt, cultures differ, but this difference confronts the locally called and formed just as much as the seminary trained. Each must attend to issues of inculturation and local re-formation if and when the locale of their ministry changes. But what each does and is ordained to do is gather and reconcile in the name of Christ. What primarily distinguishes the two is the path each has followed in their presbyteral formation. What is equally true for both is the absolute need for continuing formation and education as well as rootedness in a specific community.

Our current canons recognize the full catholicity of the seminary path yet withhold its sanction from the locally formed presbyters and deacons. What we have within our church as a result is a legally sanctioned, separate and unequal presbyterate and diaconate. It may well be that such a separation, historically speaking, was crucial to the effort of garnering enough support to ensure passage of canons allowing for local presbyters and deacons. That notwithstanding, the theological unacceptability of this canonical arrangement is becoming clear. Yet there may well be other reasons for which we do not cross the threshold into canonical reform and truly provide for one order of presbyters and deacons with varying styles of education and formation. Are we withholding catholic recognition of Canon 9 orders for fear of lack of proper education and training? Or are there concerns about possible economic ramifications, such as destabilization of the pension fund, if full recognition were granted? Such fears and concerns are legitimate, but we must deal with them and resolve them rather than allow them to dictate our theory and practice of ministry.

It is inevitable and healthy that differing systems for local formation develop throughout the Episcopal Church. Local geography, history, culture, and economy are all variables that an incarnationally based theology of baptismal ministry must take into account. In other words, inculturation of the formation process will produce variations in the process particular to a given locale. (Indeed, the program *LifeCycles* is built upon such a supposition.) This is all healthy and good, so long as what is being done is consistent with and embodies what is central to the Anglican ethos. What is this Anglican ethos, or core identity? In *Liturgical Inculturation in the Anglican Communion*, scholar David R. Holeton challenges our communion to discover the

> basic glue which holds us together as Anglicans [as] . . . not the Book of Common Prayer nor even the spirit of the Prayer Book but, rather, our common will to live together as a communion of Churches acting faithfully to proclaim the gospel among every people and culture.[2]

The baptismal covenant articulates the central values of our life together. These values, I believe, offer the basic glue to hold us together in a common life without hardening into a brittle formalism that precludes growth and variety, and which eventually cracks and breaks from the stresses of ordinary life. This is a glue with wonderful elasticity. The baptismal covenant is capable of guiding the formation process, regardless of its locale: local congregations, dioceses, and seminaries.

Ordaining and Commissioning

In a relational approach to formation and ministry development, the discernment process is not determined by the calendar. Rather, discernment takes place in God's time (*kairos*), which shapes and guides our ministry development calendar (*chronos*). The primary justification for the exercise of ministry is community recognition of gifts. A process of community discernment has identified and called forth people with gifts for service, including the ministries of the presbyterate and diaconate. Acquisition of knowledge is important, but it is not the *theological* or *ecclesiological* prerequisite for exercising a God-given gift. What, then, are our expectations of the gifted before we send them forth as ordained or commissioned to exercise their gifts as ministry on behalf of and in the name of the church?

The conventional approach of Title III, Canon 7, is to ordain presbyters upon the completion of their seminary education. This custom allows easy compliance with the stipulated time for postulancy and candidacy, as well as the study necessary to demonstrate proficiency in the required academic areas. Canon 9, on the other hand, does not require a minimum period of study, but does require that the bishop and Commission on Ministry receive satisfactory evidence that candidates understand their order's office and work, have adequate knowledge of scripture, church history, and theology as set forth in the creeds and catechism, are familiar with the Book of Common Prayer, and can conduct worship appropriately.

First of all, it is necessary for the Commission on Ministry to rethink the meaning of postulancy and candidacy. One of the strengths of mutual ministry is that the local community, not the individual, ordinarily does the actual identification of gifts and calling forth into ministry. In effect, the community says to individuals, "*We* already see this gift for this ministry at work in your daily life." One potential danger of a community-based invitation is the possibility that the community will dominate the individual. To prevent that, the period of postulancy and candidacy should become the time not for the community to determine the legitimacy of the call, since its authenticity has already been determined. Rather, this is a period of preparation, where the community provides time, space, and experiences for those who have been called forth to plumb their heart's response further. Thus candidacy is not about an individual seeking to establish a justification for "her" call, but of individuals listening to their hearts for resonance to the community's call. A candidate will reflect, "This is who you say I am. Do I see this also?"

So the process of discernment guides the calendar, not the other way around. The essence of what the identified and called forth are looking to discern in their lives, as well as the congregation and the Commission on Ministry, is evidence of personal commitment to a lifelong formation process extending beyond the initial period, which is often two to three years in length. Another important area for discernment is what the canons describe as "satisfactory evidence" of understanding their office, knowledge of the church's texts, and familiarity with the Prayer Book and the liturgy.[3] Those identified for the presbyterate and the diaconate are asking themselves, "Is what the church understands by this particular ministry who I understand myself to be?" The canon provides the touchstones for this discernment. The community has declared that they see a ministry present, at least inchoately, within the person's gifts. After a fitting time for discernment, does the one who has been identified and called agree? After the initial glow of community affirmation recedes, do the embers of self-recognition for this ministry remain and burn? This is the substance of discernment that the ministry developers, in partnership with the congregation and the Commission on Ministry, are helping to midwife.

It is necessary to bear in mind that mutual ministry seeks to offer all the members of a congregation the opportunity to have their gifts identified and to form them more deliberately and fully into a ministry on behalf of Christ for the world. Those who have been identified with gifts for leading the worship life of the community have already been seen and experienced as having the gifts for these specific ministries. The community has said that these are the persons in its midst who have the gifts for gathering and reconciliation (the ministry of the presbyterate), as well as service to world (the ministry of the diaconate), and calls them forth to exercise these gifts. What is required for ordination of these ministers is a demonstrated commitment to exercise their gifts in the manner the church asks, which includes acceptance of the responsibility to lifelong formation. Lifelong formation includes, but goes beyond, lifelong acquisition of theoretical knowledge. It is more akin to education in the classical sense—willingness to follow the Spirit in the deepening and broadening of faith and knowledge for leadership.

The trap that the Commission on Ministry must avoid is understanding and applying its formation process as simply a modified seminary track on a local level. The exercise of a gift for ministry is dependent upon being identified and called forth, as well as commitment to *responsible* exercise of ministry within a community. Canon 9 identifies the content of the word *responsible* for us, when it speaks of "satisfactory evidence." To discern "satisfactory evidence" of a lifelong commitment to formation, as well as knowledge of the texts and teachings of the church, means personal commitment and competence to exercise responsibly the ministry to which someone has been called. It is important, moreover, to place this commitment and competence within a communal setting. In other words, "satisfactory evidence" pertains also to the commitment and competency of the community of ministers. How does a leader interact with, discover knowledge with, and lead with, the members of the community of faith? This larger question establishes the full and appropriate context for discerning any particular person's commitment and competence.

Another way of describing what the Commission on Ministry seeks in discernment prior to ordination, as well as commissioning of local ministries, is the ability of the community to know, tell, live, and lead the story. This is my version of the criteria offered by Stewart Zabriskie of Nevada. With presbyters and deacons we seek "satisfactory evidence" of the ability to speak well of their calling. Can the person speak of the Christian story, drawing from the texts that define us as Christians and Anglicans? Is the person living out the story in her daily life? And is the person someone who can collaboratively lead the members of her community in the liturgical celebration of this story? These are the root questions there to guide community calling and personal discernment. *Knowing, telling, living, and leading the story* provide the satisfactory evidence, I would argue, necessary for ordination and, as appropriately adapted, for commissioning as well.

---

[1] The Standing Commission on Ministry Development is proposing a substantial revision of Title III, which would, if adopted, redress many of the issues raised here with respect to Canon 9.

[2] *Liturgical Inculturation in the Anglican Communion,* edited by David R. Holeton (Nottingham: Grove Books Limited, 1990), 7.

[3] Canon 9, Sec. 3,a,1.

℘

CHAPTER NINE

Sending Forth

My parents come from small towns in Illinois, where each was the youngest of three children. As with an untold number of families, alcoholism had penetrated and wounded my father's household. Neither of my parents' families was wealthy, by any means. My maternal grandfather, among his various jobs, contracted out for harvesting; my paternal grandfather sold cars. Both grandmothers cared for their children and homes, stretching resources to make ends meet. My mother grew up worshiping most often with the Evangelical United Brethren, whereas my father, due to the tenacity of his Irish mother, received his faith within the Roman Catholic Church.

Despite the obstacles of family alcoholism, meager means, and the Korean War, my parents' generation was the first in our family to attend college. I am not sure when my parents each felt the desire to teach. My mother was drawn by the power of music to move her soul, my dad enjoyed sports and business, and both loved to be with children and youth. Yet the story is never told of their churches celebrating this call, for this story does not exist. Why? Theirs was not a ministry in the churches' eyes, but a way of making a livelihood, a career, in the world. Even if it was the Creator God who had bestowed them with their talents, skills, desires, and dreams, no one made the connection between this bestowal of grace and their response to these gifts in the decision to become teachers.

After four years of college, work, marriage, and the birth of two children, my parents were graduated. Again, their church (my mother having been received into the Roman Catholic Communion during college) did not celebrate or commission my parents for their common ministry of teaching God's children the pursuit of truth, understanding, beauty, and cooperation. Such a celebration of their teaching as ministry would have been virtually inconceivable. What the priest did was "ministry," rooted in his vocation, his calling from God. What my parents were about to do was earn a living in the world. Their life was to matriculate outside, in the secular, whereas the priest's was centered in the sacred. They were not to be ministers of Christ in God's world, they were laity doing a job. Ministry had to do with holy things within the church, carried out by religious folk such as priests and nuns. As laity, my parents held the ladder upon which the priest ascended and descended with the holy things that sustained my parents for their worldly life. The priest conversed with the holy on their behalf. Such was the life of an ordained minister: his vocation was to keep the laity in touch with sacred things in life, cared for by the ministers of the church on behalf of the laity.

Not long ago my parents retired, after having devoted the bulk of their lives to the youth of their classrooms. They taught these children as gifts from God, God's children. They invested themselves in these children's formation into mature adults who could take delight in learning and responsibility. Each child was unique and worthy of their attention. Although I never heard them describe it this way, they lived their teaching as a sacred task, for their children were holy and worthy of their undivided creative and compassionate attention. My parents gave their lives to teaching and, yet, when the time came for them to make the transition into retirement, once again the church failed to celebrate their teaching as their ministry. Nor did the church spend time with them to listen anew to God's voice, seeking to discover where the Spirit might be calling them to serve next.

A life of service on behalf of God's children has been the longest chapter in the lives of my parents. But never once was this service explicitly understood and celebrated as such within the context of the eucharist as their baptismal ministry to God's creation. Whether it was graduation from high school and the journey to college; being graduated from college with children in tow; traveling to Michigan from Illinois to accept their first teaching positions; or retiring from active teaching after a lifetime of fidelity to their calling—not once did the church gather them up into its arms of eucharistic celebration and proclaim to them, to the members of the church, and to the city in which they dwelled, that this teaching of theirs was baptismal ministry cooperating with the sanctifying and redeeming work of God's Spirit in creation.

We may only truly speak, teach, and preach about the ministry of all the baptized, when we consistently gather up, name, celebrate, and send forth again, the work of God's people in creation done on God's behalf for creation. When this is done, we begin to live as fully as God desires into the ministry we profess in our baptismal covenant. My parents had a ministry, rooted in their calling, manifested in their skills as educators in the public school system. This calling was my parents' vocation that the church was itself unable to hear. Author Frederick Buechner describes vocation in this way: "The place God calls you to is the place where your deep gladness and the world's deep hunger meet." My parents found this place, but the church never found my parents.

Ministry begins with awareness. If we are not aware of who we are and where we are, we are, quite clearly, lost. The church "lost" my parents because it never really knew them, and it was tragically inept in assisting my parents in becoming fully aware of who they themselves were.

Mutual ministry does not begin with an action, or consist of a new-fangled program. Mutual ministry is a call, rooted in a thoroughly sacramental vision of creation, to become aware of who we are and where we are. Then, and only then, can authentic ministry begin. When I lead retreats or workshops on mutual ministry with my wife, Rïse, the place we always begin is with two questions:

Whom do you believe belongs to God, and why?
Where do you think God's most holy dwelling place is?

We then proceed to reflect on Luke's parable of the Pharisee and the publican because it is a story that calls us beyond all the maps that are meant to delineate where and in whom the holy may be found. God is in the publican as well as the Pharisee— God is in everyone. God is in the home as well as the temple— God can be found anywhere. Who belongs to God? Everyone. We cannot exclude, because God does not. Love does not. Love does not know how to exclude. Where is God's most holy dwelling place? Anywhere and everywhere. This is the foundation of church and mutual ministry. The parable is all about seeing, or becoming aware of who we are and where we are—a creation saturated in God.

Richard Rohr often repeats the insight of the mystics that we do not see the world as it is, but as we are. Mutual ministry is an invitation to see the world anew through the rediscovery of our true selves. If we become aware of who we are and where we are, then we will be able to discern well how we are all called to minister in partnership with one another. Without such awareness, we stumble about and search for quick-fix programs so that we remain busy at least doing something.

Mutual ministry is not about assigning people jobs, it is about helping members of communities become aware of who they are as God's beloved. Most remarkable in the gospel stories about Jesus' baptismal self-awareness as God's beloved is the fact that he hasn't done anything yet. He hasn't accomplished any major feat. And yet, of all the things he could become aware of—his talents, his prophetic voice, his leadership skills—what he hears God saying to him in his heart of hearts is that he is beloved. Knowing this grounds Jesus' life, ministry, death, and resurrection.

Mutual ministry begins with an invitation to discover, perhaps for the first time in our lives, that we, too, are just as beloved by God—not because of anything we have done, but because of who we are. This is sacramental awareness.

Mutual ministry is inherently collaborative because we are partners with Christ as we serve with one another. The mystics tell us if we are aware of our belovedness, our Christ-ness, in our heart of hearts, we cannot help but care well for one another with the gifts we have been given. If we remain blind to this fundamental truth, we will, at the very least, fail to see and honor the presence and gifts of others in our midst.

Within mutual ministry, *ministry is transformation through acceptance*—acceptance of who we are and where we are. Utter, complete acceptance cannot help but be thoroughly transformative in a culture that always, always, makes acceptance conditioned upon some thing, even faith. Each and everyone one of us is beloved, gifted, and called to serve. Mutual ministry roots its vision of the church—and its mission—to creation in this sacramental awareness.

BIBLIOGRAPHY

Anderson, Herbert. *The Family and Pastoral Care*. Philadelphia: Fortress Press, 1984.

Bateson, Gregory. *Steps to an Ecology of Mind*. New York: Ballantine Books, 1972.

Beck, Don Edward, and Christopher C. Cowan. *Spiral Dynamics: Mastering Values, Leadership, and Change*. Malden, Mass: Blackwell Publishers, 1996.

Bianchi, Eugene C., and Rosemary Radford Ruether, Editors. *A Democratic Catholic Church: The Reconstruction of Roman Catholicism*. New York: Crossroad, 1993.

Birch, Charles, and John B. Cobb, Jr. *The Liberation of Life*. Cambridge: Cambridge University Press, 1981.

Bookchin, Murray. *The Ecology of Freedom: The Emergence and Dissolution of Hierarchy*. Revised Edition. New York: Basic Books, 1991.

Capra, Fritjof. *The Web of Life: A New Scientific Understanding of Living Systems*. Anchor Books: New York, 1996.

Clinebell, Howard. *Ecotherapy: Healing Ourselves, Healing the Earth*. Minneapolis: Fortress Press, 1996.

Crossan, John Dominic. *The Historical Jesus: The Life of a Mediterranean Jewish Peasant*. San Francisco: Harper, 1991.

Dawkins, Richard. *River Out of Eden*. New York: Basic Books, 1995.

Eisler, Riane. *Chalice and the Blade: Our History, Our Future*. San Francisco: HarperSanFrancisco, 1988.

Fischer, Norman. *Opening to You: Zen-Inspired Translations of the Psalms*. New York: Penguin Putnam, 2002.

Friedman, Edwin H. *Generation to Generation: Family Process in Church and Synagogue*. New York: The Guilford Press, 1985.

Gilligan, Carol. *In a Different Voice: Psychological Theory and Women's Development*. Cambridge, Mass: Harvard University Press, 1982.

Gutierrez, Gustavo. *A Theology of Liberation: History, Politics and Salvation*. Translated and edited by Caridad Inda and John Eagleson. Maryknoll, New York: Orbis Books, 1973.

Hafiz. *The Gift: Poems by Hafiz the Great Sufi Master*. Daniel Ladinsky, Translator. New York: Penguin Putnam, 1999.

Hoffman, Virginia. *Birthing a Living Church*. New York: Crossroad, 1988.

Jantsch, Erich. *Self-Organizing Universe: Scientific and Human Implications of the Emerging Paradigm of Evolution*. Pergamon Press, 1980.

Johnson, Elizabeth A. *She Who Is: The Mystery of God in Feminist Theological Discourse*. New York: Crossroad, 1992.

Keller, Catherine. *From a Broken Web: Separation, Sexism, and Self.* Boston: Beacon Press, 1986.

Kennedy, S.J., Robert E. *Zen Spirit, Christian Spirit: The Place of Zen in Christian Life.* New York: Continuum, 1996.

LeaderResources at www.leaderresources.org.

Margulis, Lynn, and Dorion Sagan. *Microcosmos: Four Billion Years of Microbial Evolution.* Berkeley: University of California Press, 1997.

McFague, Sallie. *Models of God: Theology for an Ecological, Nuclear Age.* Philadelphia: Fortress Press, 1987.

McKinney, O.S.B., Mary Benet. *Sharing Wisdom: A Process for Group Decision Making.* Allen, Texas: Tabor Publishing, 1987.

Ministry Developers Collaborative at www.mindevelopers.org.

Mitchell, Kenneth R. *Multiple Staff Ministries.* Philadelphia: Westminster Press, 1988.

Moltmann, Jürgen. *God in Creation.* Minneapolis: Fortress Press, 1993.

Moltmann, Jürgen. *The Spirit of Life: A Universal Affirmation.* Minneapolis: Fortress Press, 1994.

Myers, Ruth A. *Continuing the Reformation: Re-visioning Baptism in the Episcopal Church.* New York: Church Publishing Incorporated, 1997.

Nelson, James B. *Body Theology.* Louisville, Kentucky: Westminster/John Knox Press, 1992.

Nelson, James B. *Embodiment: An Approach to Sexuality and Christian Theology*. Minneapolis: Augsburg, 1978.

Nelson, James B. *The Intimate Connection: Male Sexuality, Masculine Spirituality*. Philadelphia: The Westminster Press, 1988.

Pagels, Elaine. *The Origin of Satan*. New York: Random House, 1995.

Palmer, Parker J. *To Know as We Are Known: Education as a Spiritual Journey*. San Francisco: HarperSanFrancisco, 1993.

Parsons, George, and Speed B. Leas. *Understanding Your Congregation as a System*. The Alban Institute, 1993.

Peacocke, Arthur. *God and the New Biology*. London: Dent, 1986.

Peacocke, Arthur. *Theology for a Scientific Age: Being and Becoming—Natural, Divine, and Human*. Minneapolis: Fortress Press, 1993.

Prigogine, Ilya, and Isabelle Stengers. *Order Out of Chaos: Man's New Dialogue With Nature*. New York: Bantam Books, 1984.

Ray, Thomas. "The Small Church: Radical Reformation and Renewal of Ministry." *Anglican Theological Review*. Vol. LXXX, No. 4, Fall 1998: 615-627.

Rhodes, Lynn N. *Co-Creating: A Feminist Vision of Ministry*. Philadelphia: The Westminster Press, 1987.

Ruether, Rosemary Radford. *Women-Church: Theology and Practice of Feminist Liturgical Communities*. San Francisco: Harper & Row, 1985.

Russell, John Robert, Nancey Murphey, and Arthur Peacocke, Editors. *Chaos and Complexity: Scientific Perspectives on Divine Action*. Vatican Observatory Foundation, 1997.

Russell, Letty. *Church in the Round: Feminist Interpretation of the Church*. Louisville, KY: Westminster/John Knox, 1993.

Schillebeeckx, Edward. *Church: The Human Story of God*. New York: Crossroad, 1990.

Schillebeeckx, Edward. *The Church with a Human Face: A New and Expanded Theology of Ministry*. New York: Crossroad, 1987.

Schüssler Fiorenza, Elisabeth. *In Memory of Her: A Feminist Theological Reconstruction of Christian Origins*. New York: Crossroad, 1984.

Steinke, Peter L. *How Your Church Family Works: Understanding Congregations as Emotional Systems*. The Alban Institute, 1993.

Suchocki, Marjorie Hewitt. *God, Christ, Church*. New Revised Edition. New York: Crossroad, 1989.

Swimme, Brian, and Thomas Berry. *The Universe Story*. San Francisco: Harper: 1992.

Wheatley, Margaret J. *Leadership and the New Science: Learning about Organization from an Orderly Universe*. San Francisco: Berrett-Koehler Publishers, Inc., 1994.

Whitehead, James D. and Evelyn Eaton Whitehead. *The Promise of Partnership: A Model for Collaborative Ministry.* San Francisco: HarperSanFrancisco, 1991.

Wilber, Ken. *A Brief History of Everything.* Boston: Shambhala, 2000.

Wilber, Ken. *The Eye of Spirit: An Integral Vision for a World Gone Slightly Mad.* Boston: Shambhala, 1998.

Wilber, Ken. *Integral Psychology.* Boston: Shambhala, 2000.

Wilber, Ken. *No Boundary: Eastern and Western Approaches to Personal Growth.* Boston: Shambhala, 2001.

Wilber, Ken. *The Marriage of Sense and Soul: Integrating Science and Religion.* New York: Broadway Books, 1998.

Wilson, Edward O. *The Diversity of Life.* New York: W. W. Norton & Co., 1992.

Wink, Walter. *Engaging the Powers: Discernment and Resistance in a World of Domination.* Minneapolis: Fortress, 1992.

Zabriskie, Stewart C. *Total Ministry: Reclaiming the Ministry of All God's People.* The Alban Institute, 1995.